THE ILLUSTRATED HISTORY
- Including Standard-Triumph

Other books available from Veloce -

Alfa Romeo Tipo 6C 1500, 1750 & 1900
by Angela Cherrett
Alfa Romeo Modello 8C 2300
by Angela Cherrett
Alfa Romeo Giulia Coupé GT & GTA
by John Tipler
BIGGLES! The Life Story of Captain W. E. Johns
by Peter Berresford Ellis & Jennifer Schofield
British Car Factories from 1896 - A Complete Survey
by Paul Collins & Michael Stratton
Bugatti 57 - The Last French Bugatti
by Barrie Price
Fiat & Abarth 124 Spider & Coupé
by John Tipler
The Prince & I - My Life With The Motor Racing Prince Of Siam
(Biography of racing driver 'B. Bira')
by Princess Ceril Birabongse
The Car Security Manual
by David Pollard
Total Tuning for the Classic MG Midget/A-H Sprite
by Daniel Stapleton

First published in 1993 by Veloce Publishing Plc, Godmanstone, Dorset DT2 7AE, England.
Fax: 0300 341065

ISBN 1 874105 28 6

Readers with ideas for automotive books, or books on other transport or related hobby subjects, are invited to write to the Editorial Director of Veloce Publishing at the above address.

British Library Cataloguing In Publication Data -
A catalogue record for this book is available from the British Library.

Typesetting (in Times), design and page make-up all by Veloce on Apple Mac.

Printed and bound in England.

THE ILLUSTRATED HISTORY
- Including Standard-Triumph

BRIAN LONG

VELOCE PUBLISHING PLC
PUBLISHERS OF FINE AUTOMOTIVE BOOKS

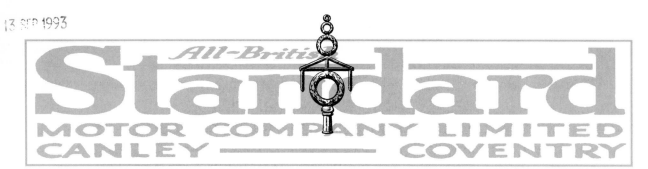

INTRODUCTION & ACKNOWLEDGEMENTS

Under the charismatic leadership of men like Reginald Maudslay and Captain John Black the Standard Motor Company, and later Standard-Triumph, grew - in a brief sixy-year lifespan - from one of Britain's pioneer motor manufacturers to one of the country's biggest car companies and car exporters in the post-war period. Along the way, Standard absorbed many other companies - including Triumph - and spread its influence far and wide.

Quite apart from producing some of Britain's and the Commonwealth's most enduringly popular cars under its own name, Standard also supplied the engines and chassis upon which were assembled SS and later the early Jaguar cars. The Company supplied components to Jensen, Morgan, Saab, TVR, Marcos, Railton, Warwick, Peerless, Fairthorpe and BRM as well as coachbuilders like Avon.

During the First World War Standard turned out many aircraft including the famous 'Harry Tate' RE8, Sopwith Pup and Bristol F2. B. In the Second World War, Standard, amongst other war work, built the Oxford Trainer and over 1000 Mosquitos. The Company also built the famous Ferguson Tractor in the postwar period.

After the Company's acquisition by Leyland Motors in 1963, Standard design and engineering lived on through the Triumph brand name in cars like the Herald, Spitfire, GT6 and 2000 and, of course, through the series of TR sports cars from TR2 to TR6.

Today, Standard cars still have an enthusiastic following and, in researching this book, I had the pleasure of meeting many people who strive to keep the name alive. Their help and advice was given freely, and I should like to acknowledge the massive contribution made by Roger Morris who, as the Chairman of the Standard Motor Club, gives up a lot of his spare time to promote the marque.

I would also like to thank Mrs Barbara Davy for all of her help. It should also be noted that her late husband's book, *The Standard Car 1903-1963*, was a constant source of reference.

Phil Homer, Tony Pingriff, Ian Leggett, Alan Withey, Chris Janes, and Mark Denton of the Standard Motor Club have my sincere thanks, as do Richard Storey of Warwick University, Steve Bagley of the Museum of British Road Transport, Roger Clinkscales, ex-Standard man Richard Levin and, last but not least, Michael Zietlin.

There are always people who one forgets to mention and to these let me say that your help is much appreciated and no less important.

I hope that you enjoy reading this book as much as I enjoyed bringing the fascinating story of Standard and Standard-Triumph together.

Brian Long, Coventry, England.

CONTENTS

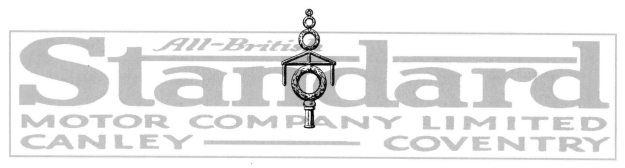

I: THE FORMATIVE YEARS

Born in Kensington, London, on the 1st of September 1871, Reginald Walter Maudslay was the great-grandson of the pioneering engineer, Henry Maudslay. It is therefore not surprising to learn that Reginald would also become involved in this field, though surely nobody could have thought it possible that this quiet young man would make such a massive impact on the British industry?

Maudslay received his education at St David's School in Moffat before enrolling at Marlborough. Later, he became an apprentice to a firm of civil engineers, and his employer at this time was none other than Sir John Wolfe Barry - the exceptional designer who is credited with, amongst other projects, the design for London's Tower Bridge. He would prove to be extremely useful in Maudslay's later years, as did Wolfe Barry's partner, Henry Marc Brunel; the son of Isambard Kingdom Brunel who engineered the Great Western Railway and was responsible for many other wonderful British landmarks. As a sign of his faith, Sir John supplied 60% of the £5,000 needed to set up Reginald Maudslay's most famous venture - the subject of this book.

Reginald, often referred to as Dick, excelled under Sir John, and played an important part in the construction of Barry Docks near Cardiff, the survey of the West Highland Railway, and several other civil engineering projects of the late 1890s. After losing his father in 1902, he moved from London to Coventry, and inspired by the motor cars he had seen in the streets of London, he decided, with the financial help of Wolfe Barry, to embark upon the manufacture of motor vehicles.

At first, premises were obtained in the so-called Conduit Yard to the rear of Smithford Street - now of course part of Coventry's City Centre. Several single- and twin-cylinder cars of various makes were purchased and examined thoroughly, and Alexander Craig was called in to put forward his design proposals for a new car, which at this time was still without a name.

Maudslay's family name was already being used by his cousins, who were also involved in the thriving Coventry motor trade. The Maudslay Motor Company was a development of the business which had been founded by Henry Maudslay nearly 100 years earlier. Based in the Lambeth area, Maudslay's factory produced literally hundreds of different marine engines, including one for the first paddle-steamer on the Thames in 1812. He had also been responsible for such ingenious designs as the micrometer and the screw cutting lathe. Sadly, Henry Maudslay died in 1831, although his sons continued to keep the family's engineering tradition very much alive.

By the mid-nineteenth century, the company had worked on steam-powered vehicles and their famous engines powered a very large percentage of the Royal Navy's ships. Business was booming, and in 1899, it was decided that a branch should be set up in the Midlands area to manufacture internal combustion marine engines.

Coventry was chosen for its engineering background, but not long afterwards the parent company in London collapsed. The Maudslay Motor Company was duly registered as a private Coventry-based firm in 1901, with Reginald Maudslay's cousins, Cyril, Charles, and Walter Henry at the helm.

Eventually, Maudslay went on to build high quality cars, commercial vehicles, and all sorts of engines for use on both land and sea. Ironically, Alexander Craig was one of the key figures in Maudslay's early history - a name that would be linked to several of the pioneering Coventry marques, including that about to be founded by Reginald.

Craig came up with many innovative designs, but unimpressed, Maudslay is said to have replied, "I don't want any of these new ideas, Mr Craig. I want my car to be composed purely of those components whose principles have been tried and tested, and accepted as reliable standards. In fact, I shall name my car the Standard car."

This does not mean that Maudslay was against any new ideas - far from it - it was just that his sound engineering experience told him that many were somewhat out of touch with reality. The proof, if it were needed, that Maudslay was not adverse to progress, comes in the Company's Articles of Association. In these, he listed the manufacture of: "Locomotive engines, cycles, boats and engines of every description, whether worked by steam, gas, oil or electricity, or any other form of power or energy, and including aerial or aeronautical machines - builders and fitters of ships and other vessels."

This showed incredible foresight, for it must be remembered that this was still only 1903, when such things as powered flight were still little more than fantasy in most people's minds.

The Standard Motor Co. was formed on the 2nd of March 1903, and a small factory in Coventry's Much Park Street was taken and equipped with £400 worth of machinery. The company's offices were registered as being 37 Earl Street, with R. W. Maudslay as the firm's Managing Director and Alexander Craig as Works Manager. Other Directors included Guy

Sir Reginald Maudslay, 1871 - 1934. Founder of the Standard Motor Company in 1903.

Archibald Maudslay, and Mr A. J. Head, the Company's first Secretary.

Reginald Maudslay was very much the man in control, however, as the minutes stated, "It was resolved that the MD have full powers as to the working of the Company, except as limited by the Articles."

It is interesting to note, that two other protégés of Sir John's became shareholders in the new company, one of whom was Alexander Gibb, the other Rustat Blake.

And so, the seeds had been sown for one of this country's most successful organisations. True, it would take time for the company to blossom, but the chapters that follow chart the many successes and failures of the Standard Motor Company, from its very first car, right through to its untimely death and the legacy it left behind ...

II: THE FIRST STANDARD CARS

Reginald Maudslay had sketched what he wanted his first car to look like during January of 1903. By the summer of that year, the sketch had turned into a reality and the first Standard car made its debut - firstly as a completed chassis (with a 6'6" wheelbase), and then as a rather unusual four-seater phaeton on receipt of its body.

Power came from a single-cylinder 6 hp engine with a bore and stroke of 5" x 3", which was mounted low down between the chassis members; underslung in effect. A three-speed gearbox was used, with a shaft drive to transmit the power to the rear axle.

For several months, this first Standard was used as an experimental test-bed, and was run without either lamps or mudguards. Although the vehicle was eventually completed and made fully roadworthy, the model was never put into production.

By the middle part of 1903, the Standard Company was employing seven people at the factory, though by the same time in 1904 this figure had increased to nearer twenty, some of whom were putting in some 70 hours per week due to the increasing popularity of the Company's work. Although the

firm now had a reasonable range of vehicles, emphasis was still given to the production of engines, and indeed, putting new engines into underpowered cars.

In 1904, a new car using a 12/15 hp twin-cylinder engine was produced, with both three- and four-cylinder machines appearing later on in the year.

The 12/15 weighed in at around 15 cwt, and this second Standard car was priced at £367. 10. 0d. It was first exhibited at the Crystal Palace Motor Show, held during February of 1904, and the first example built was later sold to Sir Alexander Gibb - a shareholder in the Company who later went on to become the President of the Institution of Civil Engineers.

By 1905, much of the original capital had been used up, though Maudslay was still receiving enough orders to keep production going at a steady rate. John Budge, who was once with the Triumph Cycle Co., and Climax Motors, was given the job of Chief Draughtsman at the Standard works during the early part of 1905.

However, not all of his time was spent in the Drawing Office, as Budge and Henry Cooper (later to be appointed the Company Secretary), set about

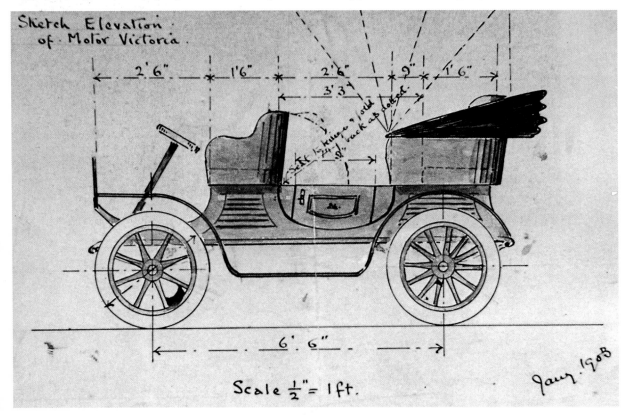

Maudslay's sketch of January 1903, clearly showing the basis for the first Standard car.

Above: The first Standard car of 1903. Christened the "Victoria", it is seen here with Alexander Craig at the wheel.

Right are two previously unpublished views of the Victoria, one showing the front of the vehicle, the other details at the rear.

putting the financial side of the business back on a firm footing after the original cashier was found to be more than a little incompetent. In fact, over £500 was brought in on uninvoiced customer repairs alone!

Rolls-Royce, Napier and Standard were among the first British manufacturers to use the six-cylinder engine. Standard's six-cylinder model, the 18/20 hp (or Standard "Six"), appearing in 1905. Continuing with Company practice, the engine could either be bought separately, or supplied with a complete chassis.

In addition to the six-cylinder car, there were also a pair of four-cylinder models; the 16/20 hp, and the 12/15 hp. At this time, the factory usually sold the

vehicles as a chassis only, although there were many different bodies available, ranging from majestic Landaulettes to Open Tourers.

1905 saw the Company make its very first export deal. A gentleman had come over to England in an attempt to buy a motor car for immediate shipment to Canada, but with very little success. On visiting the Standard factory, he was shown one of the vehicles in stock, and suitably impressed, he offered to buy the car on the spot, on the understanding that it could be shipped off straight away. A carpenter was called in to build a packing case, and the machine was on its way the very next day.

Maudslay took the decision to enter a car in the

first Tourist Trophy Race, held on the Isle of Man during September of 1905. The course was to be four rather bumpy laps totalling 208 miles, and competitors were allowed to carry just enough fuel so as to cover a minimum of 22.5 miles per gallon.

In an attempt to gain further publicity, Maudslay decided to enter a perfectly normal Standard touring car rather than a special racer - the method favoured by many of the other manufacturers - so that if the vehicle did well, it would prove beyond doubt the reliability and strength of the marque.

Wearing race number 32, the four-cylinder Standard was equipped with four forward gears instead of the usual three, giving the car a top speed of 42 mph at 1,200 rpm. Finishing in 11th place after 7 hours and 28 minutes, the Standard put up a very presentable performance, especially when one bears in mind that only 18 of the original 44 starters managed to finish at all. Unfortunately, this was to be not only the first, but also the last appearance of a Standard car in a major international motor race for a great many years.

Despite the stirling efforts of Budge and Cooper, the Company's financial position was still a little unsteady. Perhaps fortunately, the works stand at the 1905 Olympia Motor Show was visited by a certain Charles Friswell - a London-based car dealer.

Friswell stated that he could sell every vehicle that the Standard Motor Company could manufacture, and after a visit to the factory in Coventry, which now employed around 100 personnel, it was arranged that he should become the sole distributor for Standard cars in the whole of the United Kingdom.

In the last days of 1905, the Chairman reported that "after spending a considerable sum in experiments, the Company had standardised their pattern, and the cars now being built appeared to be turning out satisfactory."

It was the six-cylinder 18/20 hp model that formed the backbone of Standard car production, and from now on, it would be built in quantities of no less than ten cars per week.

Apparently contradictory confirmation of Friswell's deal was mentioned in just a single line in the Board Minutes: "London agents have also been appointed." By the simple tone of the statement, it is obvious that the Company did not realise just how important this was. Friswell stepping in when he did, almost certainly saved the Company from an early death.

In the next chapter, we'll look at the Friswell years.

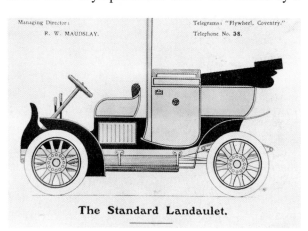

The Standard Landaulet.

Advertising from the Standard Motor Company, 1904.

A double landaulette on the four-cylinder 16/20hp chassis.

The 20hp Standard entered in the 1905 Tourist Trophy motor race.

Left; A 1905 12/15hp single landaulette. Priced at £450, a similar model on the 16/20 chassis would have cost £525.

Opposite left: The Standard car for 1904, available with either a small single- or two-litre twin-cylinder engine.

An elegant 1905 20hp model, powered by a 3.5 litre four-cylinder engine.

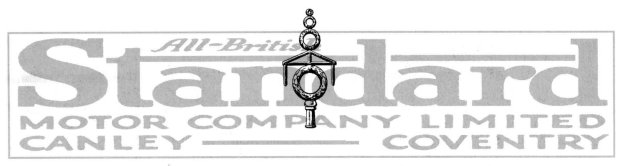

III: THE FRISWELL YEARS

A suitable number plate for the oldest surviving Standard - a 1907 30 hp model, now kept at the Museum of British Road Transport. Sammy Newsome was a well-known car dealer and racing driver.

The next oldest survivor is registered A6254; a 1908 30 hp machine with two-seater coachwork. It is pictured here some years ago at a Standard-Triumph Register event.

Charles Ernest Friswell, the son of a top London businessman, was born in December 1871 and educated privately. He was an interesting, shrewd, sort of chap, with a definite eye for spotting a good deal. As a young man, he developed his interest in cycling by setting up an agency alongside some of his other business concerns in the City. Not long afterwards, the car was brought to his attention, and in 1894, he established one of this country's first dealerships, specialising in Peugeots from France.

He took part in the famous Emancipation Run of 1896, and became well-known in motoring circles as a tough character who usually got his own way. Perhaps this is why he was chosen to head the Automobile Mutual Protection Association, a post he held for quite some time. As mentioned in the previous chapter, while Friswell was visiting the 1905 Olympia Show, he happened to call in on the Standard display. This was to be a turning point in the Company's history.

The range for 1906 included three six-cylinder cars, a four-cylinder model, and an unusual four-cylinder air-cooled vehicle, with the engine being built by W. H. Bradburn of Wolverhampton. The largest of these new Standards was the 50 hp (at £850), with the 30 hp and 18/20 making up the rest of the six-cylinder range on offer. The conventional four-cylinder machine was rated at 20 hp, whilst its air-cooled counterpart was judged to be half that figure at 10 hp.

In March 1906, Alex Craig resigned from the Company and sold all his shares. It was noted in the minutes that a loss of £1390 was made over the year,

A six-cylinder Bradburn chassis.

A light delivery van on the 15 hp chassis.

An interesting shot showing Friswell's showrooms at the time of the Imperial Press Conference, 1909.

but it was decided to write this off as the goodwill attached to the firm. Later in the same month, it was proposed that the capital of the Company should be increased from £5,000 to double that by an issue of 5,000 £1 preference shares.

Although for some reason this was never carried through, by 1907, it was again in the minds of the Directors, and was finally passed on the 18th of January, the same month in which Friswell became Chairman.

Friswell, despite being disliked by some because of his showy manner, was doubtless a fine ambassador for the Company, and indeed, the interests of the motoring fraternity in general.

For 1907, the range of production vehicles was kept very much the same, although by now, the world-famous shouldered Standard radiator had at last made its debut, and in March, there was a new 15 hp model. This new six-cylinder model was introduced to provide a relatively cheap car with a good turn of speed, and a suitable chassis for either an open or closed body.

Pridmore & Company - an old elastic weaving firm based in Coventry's Cash's Lane, had their works taken over by the Standard Company, allowing the Bishopsgate Green premises to be turned over solely to coachbuilding. A repairs and servicing department was also set up in Aldbourne Road, Coventry, and over the years, these buildings became known locally as the Widdrington Road Works.

In April 1908, Maudslay started work on a new four-cylinder 10 hp chassis, set to sell at around £200. It was hoped it would be ready for the November Show. Friswell immediately ordered six for his London outlet, but by July, the request had been changed in favour of 16 hp models fitted with Dunlop tyres. Although 10 hp models were back in the order book in November, they never appeared until much later on in the Company's history.

Late in 1908, the Union Jack-style radiator badge appeared, and this was used on all Standard cars until the end of 1930. For 1909, a new six-cylinder 20 hp car was added to the existing Standard range, which had remained virtually unchanged since 1906. A 40 hp model also made its debut, although the old 50 hp (at Friswell's request), continued to be the flagship of the fleet until it was discontinued in 1912.

The option of changing the Standard name altogether was considered in the April of 1909. Although none of the numerous suggestions were listed in the Minute Books, it is a fair bet that the Friswell name would have been in there somewhere!

By 1909, the 20 hp cars had undergone a vast number of improvements, both mechanically and cosmetically. At every opportunity, Friswell put Standard cars into the limelight. Twenty of the new 20 hp six-cylinder machines were provided for the Imperial Press Conference in 1909. Shortly after, Friswell was given a Knighthood in the birthday honours list.

Another £10,000 was raised in a Debenture Issue during February 1910, and by the year end, profits of almost £7,000 had been recorded.

Sir Charles' next big publicity stunt came in 1911, when he sailed to India with a view to providing cars for the Delhi Durbar. After much negotiation, an order for seventy cars was placed. HM King George V and Queen Mary used a splendid 20 hp landaulette finished in Royal blue with red coachlines, whilst the official cars for the Indian Government were painted an attractive cream colour.

The Durbar was a great success for the Company, but as time went by, Reginald Maudslay and John Budge found themselves with conflicting ideas to what Friswell wanted, with the situation getting more and more unbearable with each passing day.

Eventually, Friswell offered to buy out Maudslay completely, but keen to hold on to the company which he had founded, the latter made a counter-offer for Friswell's stake in the business. A Coventry solicitor by the name of C. J. Band, and several other local individuals rallied round in support of Maudslay, and quickly raised enough capital to back up the offer.

One of the people involved in the buy-out was Siegfried Bettmann, a German Jew who had (rather ironically), founded the Triumph Cycle Company. Bettmann went on to build Triumph cars as well of course, but was also Chairman of the Standard Motor Company for a while, as well as the Lord Mayor of Coventry in the years leading up to the First World War.

After a certain amount of thought, Charles Friswell conceded and left the Company in November 1912 to pursue some of his other business interests, notably in South Africa, and nearer home in Sheffield. He was paid up to the end of September 1912, and had little else to do with the Company, except sell their cars. The arrangement was made clear in a letter to Sir Charles from Maudslay, dated the 29th of October;

Dear Sir,

In consideration of your agreeing to take thirty 15 hp motor cars to be delivered as and when required within the period of four months from this date, we agree:-

(1) Not to supply any motor trader in London or within 16 miles thereof with any motor car for a period of four months from the date hereof, and

(2) Not at any time hereafter to use or mention in any advertisement or circular the name of Sir Charles Friswell or Friswells Limited.

Signed, R. W. Maudslay.
pp The Standard Motor Company.

Maudslay, it must be said, was not a great decision maker, and this is probably what led to the rift between himself and Friswell, as the latter knew exactly what he wanted, and when he wanted it.

Without the leadership qualities of Sir Charles, the Company could have faltered, but at least the support of Bettmann was a massive thing in Maudslay's favour. And so, with Friswell and Standard parting company, yet another interesting era in the Company's history came to an end. Atten-

A 1909 six-cylinder model with a rather sporty-looking four-seater touring body.

A 1910 Standard double coupé. The coachbuilt body was of an exceptionally high quality.

Below is Charles Friswell pictured in a Standard motor car during a visit to Versailles, 1909.

A six-cylinder Model L 25 hp three-quarter landaulette from late 1911.

*A 20 hp shooting brake built for Lord Harwood in 1911, and below,
the 15 hp double torpedo, November 1911.*

Left: HM King George V chatting to his chauffeur during a quiet moment on the Delhi Durbar. It was a testament to Friswell that the Royal Family chose Standard cars over their more familiar Daimler models for the occasion.

The picture below shows a 1912 six-cylinder limousine. Despite their excellent quality, it is sad to reflect that very few have survived to this day.

tions could now be turned to building cars again.

New 20 hp models were introduced in 1911 and 1913 respectively, and in 1912, there also followed new 15 and 25 hp cars, the former being christened the Model K. However, these were to be surprisingly shortlived, and Standard went into the War with a two car policy; the 1913-style 20 hp, with its 3.3 litre four-cylinder engine, and a totally new machine known as the Model S.

During 1912, the so-called "Light Car" became the fashionable way to travel. Naturally, this was quite a lucrative market, as it brought motoring within the reach of a far greater number of people than previously possible. Slightly later than some other manufacturers, the Standard Motor Company introduced their version of the light car, the Model S, in March of 1913.

Out of interest, it should be noted that Friswell's London dealership closed down for good in 1915, and he died in December 1926. The Pytchley Autocar Company took Friswell's place as the London agents in 1913, following the agreement made in October of the previous year.

The next chapter, thankfully quite free of politics, follows the development of the Standard light car - one of the most important vehicles in the Company's history, as it started the firm's shift from larger machines to smaller and more economical family cars.

IV: THE STANDARD LIGHT CAR

The so-called Light Car first became fashionable towards the end of 1912. Morris and Singer were amongst the first of the British car manufacturers to enter the field, though by the March of 1913, Standard had announced their own version of this popular new mode of transport.

Known as the 9.5 hp Model S, the Standard Light Car was put into full-scale production during August 1913, and employed a small monobloc four-

version had a two-piece windscreen, sidescreens, and a far higher quality hood - just right for the British climate! For £250, the Hurlingham Victoria was the ultimate variation on a theme, and could also be supplied with electric lighting for the modest sum of £20 extra. The Ranelagh and Richmond models were both priced at £275, and represented the very best in luxurious small car motoring.

In the meantime, the Company's capital was

A 1913 9.5 hp Model S with Rhyl two-seater coachwork. This particular car still exists today.

cylinder engine of just 1,087cc. A number of body styles were available, including the Rhyl two-seater, the Rhyl Special All-Weather, the Hurlingham Victoria, the Ranelagh Coupe, and the Richmond Fixed Head Coupe.

It was the Rhyl two-seater that proved the most popular, almost certainly because of its low purchase price. For £195, the owner received a well-engineered motor car with a comparatively large body for two, and basic protection against the elements.

Further up the range, at £210, the All-Weather

increased to £30,000 through an issue of Ordinary Shares, and an agency was established in Russia during the early part of 1913. A number of cars were shown at the St Petersburg Exhibition in that year.

More land was rented at Bishopsgate Green, as well as in the Widdrington Road area. Negotiations over some land adjoining Foleshill Road were also entered into, so it was obvious that the Company was doing well. By the end of the year, its capital had been increased to £50,000, and in the early part of 1914, it was converted into a public company.

The machine shop at the Widdrington Road Works, pictured shortly before the outbreak of the First World War. The scale of the firm's operations at this time can be judged by the number of people working on the belt-driven lathes.

Early mass-production methods at work - the building up of Standard rear axles. On close inspection, files can be seen on the benches, used by the fitters to take off any rough edges on castings or machined parts.

The small Standard was a great success, both on the home market and overseas, and further recognition came in the 1914 RAC Light Car Trials. Just one Standard was entered, but it did the Company proud by gaining a Gold Medal and by being one of only eight to finish the event.

In August 1914, a Model S chassis was successfully adopted as the basis for Standard's very first commercial vehicle. Priced at £205 with electric lighting priced at just under £16 extra, it proved to be a useful sideline to the firm's mainstream business.

Due to increased costs, the price of the Light Car was put up by £10 in February 1915, and extras went up by 5%. A total of 1,933 Model 'S' chassis had been produced by the time production was halted for war work (in May 1915), marking quite an achievement for the Company.

The chapter that follows looks into the massive effort made by the Standard Company during the Great War.

1913 9.5 hp Model S with the popular Rhyl two-seater body. At least a dozen 9.5 hp cars have survived to this day, the vast majority of them being this model.

Standard cars a generation apart; on the left, a 1936 Ten, and to the right, a 1913 Rhyl, photographed at Canley pre-WWII. [Sorry about the handwriting, unfortunately it's on the original print].

Another 1913 9.5 hp model, but this time with the Hurlingham Victoria body.

The 1913 Brighton Torpedo.

Engine building the Standard way,
with fitters working on a number of
six-cylinder power units.

Another large pre-WWI machine, also dating from 1913.

A 1913 Colonial Standard with an interesting 4wd conversion, and below, a delightful 1913 four-cylinder 20 hp cabriolet.

V: THE GREAT WAR

On the 4th of August 1914, Great Britain found itself at war with Germany and her allies. Over the months that followed, the horrid reality of the conflict was becoming apparent, and those who felt it would all blow over in a matter of weeks were proved to be very wrong.

Soon, industry was asked to lend a hand to the effort by turning over its factories to war work. Some of the motor manufacturers, such as Daimler, carried on building cars, fitting them with box bodies to aid military movements, but as the Standard Light Car

Female operatives hard at work in the Machine Shop situated in the Brewery, Leamington Spa.

was not really suitable, the Company turned its attentions in other directions.

By far the most important new product for the Company was the aeroplane. Still a relatively new machine, it was to play an increasingly valuable role in the War. Standard-built aircraft were constructed at the new works in the Canley area of Coventry. This was found to be necessary as the factory in Cash's Lane was far too small for this purpose. By September 1916, the Canley site was almost finished and a large number of famous Sopwith, Bristol, and Royal Aircraft Establishment-designed aeroplanes were completed before the War came to an end. Aircraft components for other constructors were also manufactured.

Slightly less glamorous, but equally important, was the production of artillery shells and other military equipment in four small workshops in Leamington Spa. This work was carried out largely by

women, as the vast majority of men had gone to France to fight in the trenches. This marked a new era for women, as up until this time, they had largely been regarded as second class citizens. In appreciation of their services, the British Prime Minister, Lloyd George, awarded women the right to vote - something previously the prerogative of men only.

The Standard Motor Company was responsible for well over 1,000 aeroplanes. The first order was for the BE.12, a Royal Aircraft Establishment (originally the Royal Aircraft Factory of South Farnborough), machine. In their terminology, BE stood for "British Experimental", whereas RE, as in RE.8, and also built by Standard, stood for "Reconnaissance Experimental".

The BE.12, developed from the BE.2 aircraft, was a very powerful machine, again a Royal Aircraft Establishment design. Introduced in 1916, the Company built fifty of them before moving on to other aeroplanes.

The Sopwith Pup formed a large part of the Company's aircraft production. Powered by an 80 hp Le Rhone engine, it was surprisingly capable, becoming a very firm favourite with its pilots.

Sometimes referred to as the Bristol "Fighter", the F.2B two-seater was a heavy machine compared with the Pup, so needed a far more powerful engine. Four different power units were employed through the aircraft's production run; the Rolls-Royce "Falcon", the 200 hp Hispano-Suiza, Sunbeam "Arab", or Siddeley "Puma". With the Standard-built machines, it was the latter two that were used.

The order for three hundred Martinsyde Buzzard fighters was cancelled due to world events, and a number of other contracts were either transferred to full-time aircraft manufacturers, cancelled or only partly completed by the Company.

On the 11th of November 1918, the world breathed a sigh of relief, as peace was at last declared. It had been an Allied victory, brought about on the Home Front just as much as in the trenches. Now, the massive task of returning to normality faced the British industry.

Immediately after the War, the Model "S" was put back into limited production. In fact, nearly 200 of these models - Standard's first volume produced car - were built during the latter part of 1918. The car that was to be its successor is the subject of the next chapter, but first we shall look in detail at the aircraft built by the Company as part of their contribution towards the War effort.

A general view of the aircraft workshops at Canley. Standard's involvement in the production of warplanes was a great help to the Allies.

The RE. 8 shop at Canley, pictured in November 1917. By this time, the Company had already applied for Government Authority to allow them to resume their ordinary trade as soon as hostilities ceased.

A BE. 12 awaiting completion at the Canley works, seen here in its younger days.

The Bristol F. 2B, this one, no.E5180, with Sunbeam power.

B6065 - a Sopwith Pup built during the latter part of 1917.

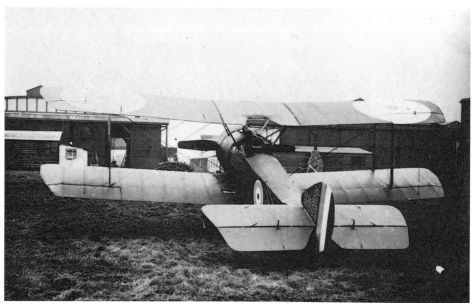

Nick-named the "Harry Tate", this is an RE. 8. Powered by a 130 hp RAF engine; Standard built over 400 of these aircraft.

Aircraft built by the Standard Motor Company during World War One

Serial No.	Qty.	Aircraft	Notes
6136 - 6185	50	BE. 12	Built for the Army.
A626 - A675	50	Sopwith Pup	Built for the Royal Flying Corp.
A4564 - A4663	100	RE. 8	Built for the Royal Flying Corp. At least two were converted to RE. 9 aircraft.
A7301 - A7350	50	Sopwith Pup	Built for the Royal Flying Corp.
B1701 - B1850	150	Sopwith Pup	Rebuilt machines for the Royal Flying Corp, although three later went to the Royal Navy.
B5901 - B6150	250	Sopwith Pup	Rebuilt machines for the Royal Flying Corp.
C201 - C550	350	Sopwith Pup	Built for the Royal Flying Corp. Some of these aircraft were completed after the War, and went straight into storage. Eleven of them were given new numbers and were then sent to Australia.
D1501 - D1600	100	RE. 8	Built for the Royal Flying Corp.
D4661 - D4810	150	RE. 8	Built for the Royal Flying Corp.
E5179 - E5252	74	Bristol F. 2B	Built for the Royal Air Force. Sunbeam Arab aero-engines used.
E5253 - E5258	6	Bristol F. 2B	Built for the Royal Air Force. Siddeley Puma aero-engines used.
E5259 - E5308	50	Bristol F. 2B	Order later transferred to the British & Colonial Aeroplane Company.
E5309 - E5428	120	Bristol F. 2B	Order cancelled.
F1665 - F1764	100	RE. 8	For the R.A.F., but completion not confirmed.
J5592 - J5891	300	Martinsyde F4 Buzzard	Order cancelled.

VI: THE SLS & SLO STANDARDS

After the highly successful Model "S", the Standard Company decided to follow its proven formula, and introduced another 9.5 hp model - the SLS. The SLS was powered by a four-cylinder engine of 1,328cc, compared to 1,087cc on the pre-war car. This slightly larger capacity was achieved by introducing a slightly longer stroke.

In two-seater form, the SLS cost £350, cheap enough to encourage many an ex-Serviceman to part with his gratuities. Although the car was undeniably reliable, highly praised by the motoring press, and perfect to get the factory back into production, it was obvious that a new machine would have to follow shortly if the Company was to remain competitive. Testing of a brand new prototype was carried out by Maudslay in the hills and mountains of Scotland and Wales during the early part of 1921.

The new 11.6 hp model, known as the SLO, was introduced in the July of 1921. It was basically the same as the SLS, but with an overhead-valve engine rather than side-valves. In fact, it should be noted that this was the first ohv Standard ever produced.

The other important feature of the SLO was its longer chassis, much more suitable for four-seater bodies. This was largely brought about by Maudslay

Standard advertising from 1920. Note the address of the London showrooms.

Below: As the original caption implies, this picture shows Standard Light Cars in the making at Canley.

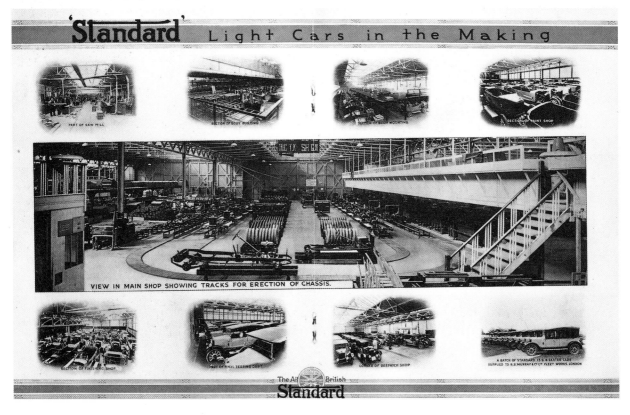

The Standard Motor Company works at Canley pictured shortly after the First World War. Ivy Cottage can be seen clearly in the top inset.

factory. It had first been seen by Maudslay at a Sotherby's auction, and nothing could have been more appropriate. The Company's works at Canley had, by this time, grown quite substantially. It now featured a separate body assembly line, and even a test track which was built around the factory perimeters. Expansion didn't stop there though, and the works continued to grow over the years that followed at what can only be described as a staggering rate.

This new production facility would be necessary for the latest new Standard, the SLO-4. This large, 13.9 hp model made its debut in the early part of 1922 and was an immediate success.

The SLO-4 offered more spacious accommodation for passengers and, for the driver, better performance . With prices starting at just £450 as well it represented excellent value for money and, rightfully, put Standard in the same league as the other big manufacturers such as Austin and Morris.

So popular was the new Standard that it became quite a common sight on the British roads, and a new advertising slogan, "Count Them On The Road" was coined. To give an idea of production figures, over 4,000 were built in 1923 alone. Fortunately for modern generations, quite a few have survived to this day in their various guises.

In 1924, a dinner was held to celebrate the 21st anniversary of the incorporation of the Company. At this time, John Budge was the Chairman, and the whole event was quite a jolly affair. Indeed, with the

himself, for as a keen owner-driver with a growing young family, he soon realised that the SLS was not the ideal car for everyone. Effective weather protection was also made a priority, and it has often been said that the SLO was the first British tourer to have a fully weatherproof hood and sidescreens. On its introduction, the cheapest SLO was priced at £515.

In the following October, the SLS was superseded by a smaller 8 hp model, available with either a two- or four-seater body. This too employed an ohv engine, though it was never particularly successful, and in the end, very few were ever built.

The main failing of the 8 hp was advanced features that were frankly under-developed. Aluminium pistons with tubular connecting rods were wasted on a crankshaft with only two ball bearings to support it. Overhead valves were fine, but the owner had to lubricate the rocker gear by hand each time a journey was made.

It is sad that such an attractive machine was so short-lived. Perhaps if the introduction had been delayed slightly, and even the price increased a little to allow for good engineering practices to be carried out, the 8 hp would have been a fine motor car.

However, in the meantime, the SLO continued to be a roaring success, demand reaching a point where shortly it would outstrip supply. A final batch of 1,000 cars was built towards the end of 1921, the final few of them carrying a new, soon to be famous, trademark.

By December of 1921, the Roman Standard of the IXth Legion was being used as a trademark by the

A contemporary view of the Finishing Shop shortly after the First World War.

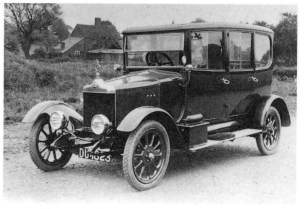

Prototype four-door saloon coachwork on the 9.5 hp SLS chassis.

An SLO chassis prepared for the Olympia Motor Show. Note the burnished surfaces and extra badges.

One of the rare 8 hp Standard chassis. The picture was taken at the 1921 Motor Show.

re-introduction of the McKenna import taxes, the British market could not have been better for the home manufacturers.

In his speech, Maudslay stated, "As to the Standard Motor Company's prospects, I am an optimist, and I am an optimist because I feel sure that we have in this Company the right spirit, the spirit not only of work, but of progress." In fact, Maudslay had every right to be optimistic, as production levels rose to around 10,000 cars for the year.

The SLO was discontinued in 1924, although the SLO-4 (or 14/40 hp), was carried over with optional four-wheel brakes, and a new 11.4 hp car - the four-cylinder Model V3 - was introduced.

Bodies available on the SLO-4 included the Leamington (a two-seater with dickey seat), the Warwick 4/5-seater tourer, the Portland saloon, and the Pall Mall saloon. A mixture of local and London names figured strongly in the bodies available on the V3 model as well, such as the Canley two-seater tourer, the Coleshill tourer, the Kineton four-seater tourer, the Kenilworth tourer, and the Piccadilly four-seater saloon.

For 1925 and 1926, the Standard range was left much the same, except the slightly larger Model V4 had been introduced, with a new 14/28 hp ohv engine. Accordingly, the Stratford and Wellsbourne (both four-seater tourers), were announced for the new model, as well as the Sidmouth tourer, the Charlecote drophead coupé, the Corley, and the Sherbourne.

Eventually, the repairs department was moved from Widdrington Road, and these buildings were later used for stocking up on spare parts. The Bishopsgate Green works were converted for sheet metal work, and the factory in Cash's Lane became used for all of the firm's machining operations. Canley

A 1921 four-seater 8 hp model. The two-seater was priced the same at £325.

was still the main works though, by this time covering over 400,000 square feet.

As time went by, four-wheel brakes became the norm and by the end of 1925 the Company was listing them as standard equipment across the board.

The General Strike, held in support of the plight of coal miners, lasted from the 3rd to the 12th of May, 1926, and was basically a sign of the times - a warning of what was to come. Sales dropped slightly, as there simply wasn't the same money around as there had been only a few years earlier.

However, the Company decided to ignore all the tell-tale signs of an economic recession and in 1927 introduced its first post-war six-cylinder model; the 18/36 hp, or 6-V. Although this was an exceptionally nice motor car, it was too big and expensive for the market at that time.

Fortunately, the smaller cars were continued alongside the 18/36, and it soon became evident that the timing of the new car's launch could not have been worse.

Financial help from the Company's bankers enabled them to continue trading through this difficult period, and stave off two separate attempts by the Rootes brothers to take over the Company. However, the decision to revert to smaller machines built in large numbers was undoubtedly the factor that prevented collapse of the business.

The next chapter looks at the Wall Street Crash's effect on the Company's policy decisions.

The 13.9 hp Standard outside the Moor Park Golf Club, pictured in 1924.

A typical rural garage scene from the early 'twenties, with Standard to the fore.

*A 1921 SLO with typical
two-seater coachwork.*

*The Kineton four-seater
touring body on a 1924
11.4 hp Model V3 chassis.
Several similar examples
have survived to this day.*

*The Coleshill two-seater
tourer on the V3 chassis,
again from 1924.*

A Stratford four-seater tourer based on the SLO-4 - one of several superb examples still on the road today.

This is the Warwick body on the 13.9 hp SLO-4 chassis, seen at the old Standard works.

VII: 1927 to 1935

The 1926 General Strike had far reaching effects on almost all of British industry, and the Standard Motor Company was no exception. By 1927, like so many car manufacturers, the business was in fact struggling to remain bouyant, and the firm's bank was ready to liquidate the Company.

Indeed, had it not been for William Morris threatening to withdraw his substantial deposits from his and Maudslay's bankers, the Standard Motor Company may well have died off there and then. Instead, a compromise was reached by appointing E. J. Corbett of Barclays to the Board, and a new Chief Engineer, Alfred Wilde.

In reply to these worsening times, the Company decided to continue with the 11.4 hp V3 and 13.9 hp V4 models, but also introduced a pair of new Standards; the larger 18/36 hp Model 6-V, and fortunately, a far smaller 8.9 hp Standard "Nine."

The Model 6-V, as noted in the previous chapter, employed a six-cylinder ohv engine, and was available with a variety of saloon and touring bodies, but it was the delightful little Nine which stole the limelight.

Launched at Olympia late in '27, the "Worm-Drive Nine" used a four-cylinder inclined side-valve engine, and had gone from Wilde's drawing board to production in less than six months. Despite this hurried introduction, however, the car was "right" virtually from the start - the engine being one of the Company's most important technical developments pre-war.

Two prototypes had been built, and were run twenty-four hours a day around the Cotswolds for one month. During this severe testing, they averaged just over twenty-five miles per hour, and returned between thirty-five and forty miles to the gallon. At the end of their trial, only around £5 worth of spares were needed to put the cars back in their original

A Gordon England model, dating from 1928, racing at Brooklands - a sports car based on the Nine.

condition - not bad at all after over 18,000 miles.

The car's designer, Alfred Wilde, had a brilliant career, sadly cut desperately short through ill health and exhaustion from overwork. Born in 1891, he died at just 39, but in this short life he worked on artillery pieces, aircraft engines and, finally, motor cars.

Originally working with the small Seabrook outfit in London, he moved to Hotchkiss of Coventry when the former closed down. After the Hotchkiss works were sold to Morris, Wilde moved to Paris, but soon returned to Coventry after being offered a position with Standard.

His talents were typified by the Nine. It was the Falmouth fabric-bodied saloon that was first made available to the public and, selling at just £198,

THE 12/24 H.P. "WELLESBOURNE"
5-Seater

THE 12/24 H.P. "PARK LANE"
Saloon

it became very popular straight away.

The Nine was naturally continued for the 1928 season and, thanks to its immediate success, was made available with a variety of bodies; there were two- and four-seater tourers, the Falmouth and Fulham fabric-bodied saloons, and special two-seater saloons or sports cars by Gordon England, these models having the added option of a supercharger. A fabric saloon body known as the Farnham augmented the V4 range, and the V3 was at last dropped from the model listings.

The recently-introduced Model 6-V was continued virtually unchanged, though slightly later on in the year it was joined by another variant; the 18/24 hp. This had the same engine as the 6-V, but was equipped with a four-speed gearbox, and had horizontal bonnet louvres as opposed to the vertical ones found on the 18/36. In view of the economic climate this seems like certain suicide but, somehow, the Company's success in the small car market carried them through.

In August 1928, the sharp lines of the saloon bodies were rounded off slightly to give a more pleasing appearance, and the chassis was lowered by two inches. During September a 9.9 hp version of the "Nine" was introduced. It was basically a long wheelbase 8.9 hp model with a slightly bored-out engine, and the first model to be marketed on this new chassis was the Teignmouth fabric-bodied saloon.

There was much success for the Company in trials and races during 1928. The two-seater "Sports" models appeared at Brooklands - seven of them

A typical fabric-bodied 1928 Standard. This one on the Nine chassis, inspired by the contemporary Mathis.

entering the JCC High Speed Trial over 115 miles, including one supercharged Gordon England model.

For 1929, the 8.9 hp car was continued as it had been in the previous year, although the 9.9 hp Teignmouth was joined by a steel-bodied coachbuilt Teignmouth saloon and the Selby four-seater tourer. A 15 hp "Fifteen" Exmouth fabric saloon made its debut, as did the six-cylinder 1,930cc Envoy and Ensign steel saloons. Later on in the year, the 16 hp "Sixteen" with a six-cylinder 2,054cc side-valve engine was announced. This, at least for its first year, carried so-called Tourist Coupé bodywork.

Other interesting developments during 1929, included a link with the Jensen brothers in the Spring,

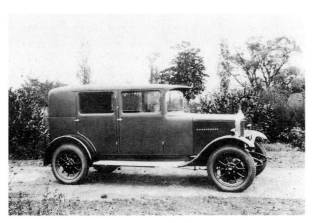

A 1928 14/28 hp Farnham fabric saloon.

1929 Tourist Coupé on the 9.9 hp chassis.

The 9 hp Selby four-seater.

A 1929 9.9 hp four-light Teignmouth.

The coachbuilt version of the Teignmouth, this example dating from 1930.

A 1930 Standard Nine with a Fulham fabric body, and below, an Avon Special in friendly competition.

and also a link with the Swallow coachbuilding concern - the company co-founded and owned by William Lyons, of course.

The story behind the Jensen brothers and their first contact with Standard is a particularly interesting one, as it involved the Avon coachbuilding concern as well. The Jensen-designed "Avon Special" was a joint project between the two brothers, Allan and Richard, and Avon. This was because, at this time, the Jensens had not got the finance to take on the whole venture themselves, so needed the established concern to put up colateral as much as their technical know-how. It was a superb motor car, and although the Jensens went their own way shortly after, the Standard and Avon names would be linked together for a long time to come.

As predecessor to the world famous Jaguar Cars Ltd, the Swallow Coachbuilding Company will always have a very special place in the history of the British motor car industry. Although various chassis were used by William Lyons, it was the Standard Nine that first brought the Company and Lyons together. The first Standard-Swallow appeared in October 1929, and sold for just £235 in two-door form.

For 1930, the Standard range was reduced to the 9.9 hp "Big Nine", introduced to replace the previous two "Nine" models, and the 15 and 16 hp cars. Both two- and four-seater saloon and touring bodies were available on the Big Nine, as well as the specialist coachbuilt bodies by the likes of Avon and Swallow. An interesting modification was the spiral bevel rear axle in place of the old worm-driven one. The 15 hp Exmouth and Ensign models were continued unchanged, although the name Envoy was passed on to the larger 16 hp car.

Prices ranged from £185 for a 9 hp Fulham saloon, to £365 for the Envoy Special, fitted with wire wheels and numerous other luxuries. *The Autocar* described the Envoy as a "remarkable car for the money, and one that functions well in every respect."

The 1931 season cars, the last built under A. H. Wilde's supervision, lost their distinctive shouldered radiator grille and Union Jack badges, in an attempt to bring the cars more in line with their more modern-looking competitors. The new range, which included last year's Big Nine and Exmouth, a 16 hp Ensign using the 1930 Envoy engine, and a new 2,552cc six-cylinder 20 hp model using the Envoy name, continued to sell well all over the world, despite being slightly more expensive than the rival Austin, Morris, and Hillman models.

The Avons and Swallows almost certainly helped to boost both the Company's image and sales, but with cars going all over the Continent, and even the Far East, there can be no denying the popularity of the vintage Standard car. One of the key figures behind this new-found energy in the Company was Captain J. P. Black .

Born in Kingston, Surrey, in 1895, John Black trained as a lawyer in his early days. In the Great War, he joined the RNVR and survived the Gallipoli assault. Later, he asked for a transfer to the Tank Corps, and saw action in France. When demobbed in 1919, he held the rank of Captain.

After the War, he went to the Hillman concern of Coventry, and although he was never really liked there, he earned the respect of his workforce, and even married one of William Hillman's daughters. However, in 1929, Black joined the Standard Motor Company as joint MD with Maudslay, injecting it with fresh capital and, more importantly perhaps, fresh ideas. Black saw immediately the benefits of supplying chassis to the likes of Avon and Swallow, and nurtured the relationship in a way that suited the Company best.

The range for 1932 included an 8.9 hp Little Nine introduced alongside the 9.9 hp Big Nine. The Little Nine used a new short-stroke 1,006cc engine, and a number of coachbuilt saloons were made available, as well as two- and four-seater tourers.

The 16 hp "Sixteen" (the former Ensign), and 20 hp "Twenty" (the former Envoy), were continued. Both the 9 and 16 hp chassis were supplied to Avon and Swallow, and the 16 hp was also supplied to Mulliner, who produced an attractive four-door close-coupled saloon. Prices at this time ranged from £145 for the Little Nine tourer, to just over twice that for the Twenty. The Mulliner-bodied car, incidentaly, sold at £255.

The Works Pavillion at Canley was opened by HRH the Duke of Gloucester during July of 1932. The Duke, himself a notable supporter of the Standard marque, taking delivery of a 1933 model "Sixteen" saloon as if to prove the point, spent most of the day with his hosts, Maudslay and Black.

During the same month, two new Standard models made their debut; the so-called "Little Twelve", and naturally, the "Big Twelve". These used a six-cylinder side-valve engine, and both saloon and touring bodies were available on the new chassis.

The Standard Motor Company had managed to buck the Depression with keen pricing, and a reputation for solid reliable cars. Competition successes were again numerous during the early years of the 1930s, particularly at Brooklands, and in the RAC and Monte Carlo Rallies. An Owners Club was also formed in 1932 to bring together the many enthusiasts who used their vehicles for sporting occasions.

The 1933 Standard range continued as for 1932, with most of the activity being centred around the specialist coachbuilders. The Jensen Brothers decided to end their association with Avon, and joined forces with Patrick Motors of Birmingham to produce the Bournebrook Special - a four-seater sports tourer on the Standard Little Twelve chassis.

Avon hired the designer Charles Beauvais to fill the gap left by the Jensens, and his tourers, coupés, and saloons on the 9 hp and 16 hp Standard chassis were outstandingly pretty. One of the most important innovations introduced by Beauvais was his flashing direction indicators - a feature found on every new car built today.

In the meantime, William Lyons was in the process of launching the superb series of "SS" cars.

The 1932 Little Nine saloon, initially priced at just £155. The 1933 model had a flatter roof and a new wing line.

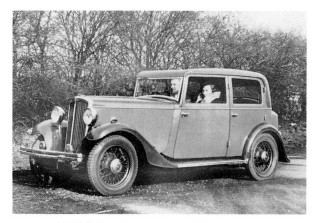

A 1933 Dorchester on the 16 hp chassis.

1933 Twenty landaulette, with elegant coachwork by Mulliners of Birmingham.

The 1934 model year Standard Twelve saloon.

A delightful picture showing the 1934 Standard Ten.

The 1934 Sixteen De Luxe saloon, and below, a 16 hp tourer from the same period.

Nobody really knows exactly what SS stands for (Standard-Swallow being the likeliest possibility), but anyone with the slightest interest in motor cars knows what it means - long, low and elegant sports cars.

Due to be introduced in 1932, the SS1, based on the Standard Sixteen chassis, was hurriedly brought forward to make a stunning debut at the 1931 Motor Show, along with the SS2 produced on the Little Nine. By 1933, the Coventry-built range of SS cars was identified as a new marque, totally independent, even though chassis were still supplied by Standard.

Perhaps the finest compliment for Lyons' firm was the order received from Captain Black who wanted a 20 hp tourer for himself. It was duly delivered in the March of 1933, one of the first of its kind.

The 20 hp chassis was used by Mulliners for their dignified landaulettes and seven-seater saloons, and Midland Light Bodies Limited produced an ambulance on the same Standard frame. During the summer of 1933, John Black was appointed as the Company's new Managing Director, a position which he had held jointly for a while with Reginald Maudslay himself - Chairman and Founder of the Company.

Ted Grinham joined Standard, like Black, after previously being with the Rootes Group. He was given the job of Chief Engineer, and actually designed the "Little Nine" and the 1934 "Nine" and "Ten". Much planning had gone into the '34 range, and over 1,500 Standard agents were invited to the Canley works to inspect the cars. This must have been a great success, as large orders were taken from the agents, filling the order books both at home and

A two-door version of the Nine. Priced at £145, it was £20 cheaper than the four-door model.

The 1935 four-door Nine, also available in De Luxe form for just £10 extra.

overseas. By the October of 1933, a net profit of no less than £132,000 was announced.

For 1934, the 9 hp Nine replaced the previous Little Nine, and the 10 hp Ten took over from the outdated Big Nine. Both the Nine and Ten were available as either saloons or tourers - the Nine as a two- or four-door saloon, and the Ten with a drophead coupé model alongside the four-door saloon. Prices ranged from £135 for the basic Nine to £168 for its 10 hp stablemate, although both models could be supplied to De Luxe specification at extra cost.

Other cars for 1934 included the 11.9 hp four-cylinder Twelve, the 13.5 hp six-cylinder Fourteen (or more correctly Twelve-Six, for it was a larger engine fitted in the Twelve chassis), the Sixteen, and the Twenty.

The 10/12 hp Speed Model saloon was introduced in the spring of 1934, which combined the new

11.9 hp four-cylinder side-valve engine from this year's Twelve in the 10 hp chassis. A "Sport Coupé" was also produced in two-seater form, but it was the elegant closed "Speedline" model that was really striking. It had more than a hint of the SS Airline in it, and gave buyers a taste of the "Flying Standards" that would follow in due course.

Two 10/12 Speed Models were entered on the RAC Rally, and although they did not feature strongly, they did at least finish the event. Top speed was put at seventy-two miles per hour, a very impressive performance for such a car in the immediate post-vintage period.

Avon produced some delightful fixed- and drophead coupés on the 10 hp chassis, and sports saloons on the 16 hp chassis. Salmon and Son (Tickfords), also produced a drophead coupé based

1935 four-door tourer on the LWB Nine chassis. It was priced at £165.

The Tickford Foursome Coupé from the same year, with prices from £245 to £365.

The Standard Speed 10/12 shown in both saloon and coupé form. The 10/12 hp engine is shown in the inset to the right.

on the 10/12 hp - the so-called "Speed Special" model. The first Atlas commercial appeared, being a van body on the four-cylinder 12 hp chassis. At the other end of the scale, HM King George V ordered a Standard Twelve for the use of servants at Windsor, and the Prince of Wales was often seen being driven in a Twenty landaulette whilst in the Midlands area.

1934 was to see Reginald Maudslay preside over his last AGM. Sadly, the great man died at the end of the year, aged just 64. Once described as a "gentlemanly engineer of the old school", he left a wife and three children.

Despite problems with several important suppliers, 1934 went on to be a record year so far as sales were concerned. In fact, C. J. Band noted, such was the demand for Standard cars, that because of these troubles, some orders had gone unfulfilled. However, 20,000 cars found new homes in 1934.

The 1935 range was largely the same as it had been in 1934 except the 9 hp model was made available in four-door form. The 10/12 hp model became available as a Sports Saloon, Sports Coupé, or Speedline Saloon which, as mentioned earlier formed the basis for the future Flying Standards.

Tickford folding heads were listed for both the 10/12 Speed and the basic Ten chassis and, naturally, there were the Avon cars. Avon now gave names to their models, producing the Waymaker sports saloon in pillarless form on the 16 hp chassis, and the Waymaker II (identical to the Waymaker except for a shorter bonnet), on the 10/12 hp Speed chassis.

Samuel Holbrook Limited of Wolverhampton produced the angular Dorchester saloon on the larger 16 hp chassis, and then there was the SS range, which

The elegant lines of the 1935 10/12 Speed coupé, with coachwork by Carbodies of Coventry.

Another of the 1935 models, and perhaps the most attractive, this is the Speedline four-seater.

had by now matured into a fine British make.

So far, SS had employed the Ten, Twelve, Sixteen, and Twenty chassis for their cars, which included saloons, tourers and drophead coupés. The SS90, though, of 1935 vintage, was a two-seater sports car, and provided the basis for the legendary SS100. The latter continued to use the Weslake-tuned 2,663cc Standard engine, but now an in-house-designed chassis, built by Rubery Owen, was employed.

There were more extensions to the Canley works during the Spring of 1935, and it was announced that sales were up a further 20% on the previous year. The factory now had a number of conveyor systems installed to aid production, and even an overhead electric tram to bring bodies from the line to the Paint Shop. It was estimated that a car could be completed roughly every three minutes with this new highly-mechanised set up, but 150 cars a day was considered to be the norm.

The 1936 range was announced in August 1935, and included no real surprises, probably because of the massive changes planned for the following year.

There was the two-door Nine with its 1,052cc four-cylinder engine. This was priced at £135, or £155 in De Luxe form. The four-door Nine was £169, with its body being mounted on a slightly longer wheelbase. The 1,343cc four-door Ten was priced at £189, and the Light Twelve - a 1,608cc 12 hp engine in a Ten chassis, commanded £195. The Standard Twelve model was priced at £229.

Onto the six-cylinder cars: there was the 2,143cc Sixteen at £269, the Light Twenty; a 2,663cc 20 hp engine in the Sixteen chassis at £275, and the standard Twenty at £395. The latter could also be supplied with a longer wheelbase for coachbuilders at £450.

All of the Company's 1935 models, except the basic Nine, were supplied in De Luxe form only

Enthusiasm for the Standard marque was high in the mid-'thirties ...

... with many trials and other events being organised for Standard owners.

HRH Prince Philip's first car, a 1935 Standard Nine.

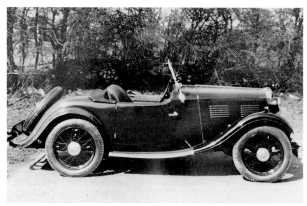

A pretty little Sports Tourer on the 9 hp chassis.

The prototype 9.9 hp Avon Special, designed by the Jensen brothers.

An Avon advertisment for the 1932 trading season. Note how many models they listed.

Avon at the 1931 Olympia Motor Show.

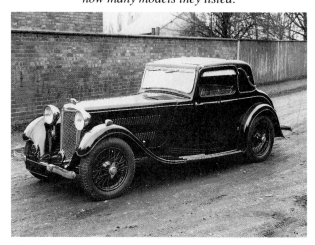

The Beauvais-styled Avon coupé mounted on the 1933 16 hp chassis.

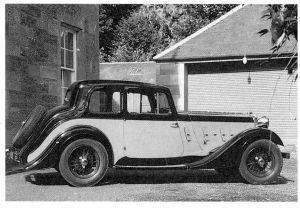

Another 16 hp Avon, this one dating back to 1934, and a survivor to this day.

A 1935 sports saloon by Avon. It was built on the 12 hp chassis.

The 1936 model year Standard Twenty, with tasteful six-light coachwork.

although, for just £20 extra, this could easily be arranged on the Nine as well. Leather-trimmed seats, sliding roofs, a synchromesh gearbox, and electric windscreen wipers were the order of the day.

By offering the public good reliable cars at reasonable prices, the Standard Motor Company managed to get past this awkward period that saw the end of many motor manufacturers from across the world - indeed, if anything, the marque became stronger.

The following chapter looks in depth at what new models the Company were going to sell over the next five years, and what they were doing in preparation for the forthcoming conflict ...

VIII: THE FLYING STANDARDS

Although the 1936 range had been announced in the August of 1935, three cars had been held back until the '35 Olympia Motor Show. Captain Black stated that they would bring the Company "even greater success and prosperity" over the coming years.

Fortunately, Black was to be proved right, as these new models, christened the "Flying" range, were immensely successful for well over a decade. The smallest of the Flyers was the 12 hp Flying Twelve. It had a four-cylinder 1.6 litre engine, a nine foot wheelbase, sold for £259, and was easily capable of 70 miles an hour.

The 16 hp six-cylinder 2.1 litre Flying Sixteen was the next in the line-up. This was priced at £299 and judged to be capable of 75 miles per hour, whilst the 2.7 litre 20 hp Flying Twenty was sold for £315, for which the owner had 80 mph performance. Both the Flying Sixteen and the Twenty had a 9'8" wheelbase.

Visually, the Flying Standards were a hit, and they were every bit as good on the road as they looked. One magazine described the Flying Twenty chassis as an "excellent performer on the road, for it has swift and smooth acceleration, and an easiness of running over the flats or up the hills that has to be experienced to be appreciated."

Avon coachwork took the Flying range from tasteful to verging on the exotic. Naturally, a far higher cost was involved, with prices starting at £335, going on to £370 for the coachbuilt Flying Twenty.

Later on in the year, other Flying Standards became available - March 1936 saw the 10 hp Flying Ten make its debut, along with the 12 hp Flying Light Twelve. These were priced at £199 and £205 respectively to bring them in line with competition, and used the same cruciform underslung chassis. The only difference was naturally in the engine size; the 10 hp model having a 1.3 litre unit and the 12 hp model a 1.6 litre engine.

October 1936 saw the launch of the 9 hp Flying Nine, along with a number of other Flying Standards, including a new Flying Ten, a Flying Fourteen, and a V-8 powered 20 hp. The Flying Nine was a two-door saloon, whilst all the other standard Flyers were four-door machines. It was fitted with a 1,131cc four-cylinder engine, and priced from £149.

The new Flying Ten had a 1,267cc power unit as opposed to the old 1,343cc one, and was £20 more expensive. The Flying Twelve's engine remained the same 1,608cc, but the old Ten engine was made available as an option.

The Flying Fourteen could have either the

The prototype Flying Twelve of 1935, trimmed slightly differently on each side for evaluation by the Board. Right, a rear view of the same car. It was designed by Frank Salter, Ted Grinham and Alfred Wilde.

Twelve engine or its own 1,776cc unit, and likewise, the Flying Twenty could have the old Sixteen engine, or its own 2,663cc six-cylinder one.

By far the most interesting of these new models was the other Flying Twenty - the V-8. Priced at £349, this 2.7 litre machine was not cheap, but it fascinated visitors to the show stand at Olympia. It was the second V-8 the Company had shown, the first appearing briefly in 1921, and was based on two 10 hp blocks welded together in a Vee.

Capable of over eighty miles per hour, it was the first of the Flying models to be fitted with the famous waterfall radiator grille. Sadly, it was not to everyone's taste, and very few saloons were built, even less of the rare drophead versions, priced at just £10 more.

Avon continued with their own models on the 12, 16, and 20 hp chassis (either basic or Flying spec), and Mulliner produced a diminutive two-door landaulette on the 9 hp chassis. SS models continued much the same but by now, the Jaguar name had been introduced.

In the meantime, Captain Black had been involved in discussions with Whitehall officials over the probability of war, and what the country could do to defend herself if indeed war did break out. Also involved were Daimler's Sir Geoffrey Burton, Spencer Wilks of Rover, Lord Austin, William Rootes, and Alfred Herbert, the famous engineer. The Shadow Factory Scheme was initiated, and towards the end of 1936 Black unveiled the building plans that were to be undertaken to the rear of the existing Canley factory.

The 1937 RAC Rally saw nine Standard cars entered. This can be broken down into seven Flyers, a 12 hp drophead coupé, and a basic Nine which won a coachwork award.

New showrooms were established in Mayfair in London during mid-1937 to cope with the increased demand, and it was at this time that the Fourteen and Twenty Touring Saloons were introduced. These had a larger luggage capacity than usual, and were priced at £279 and £329 respectively.

The Autocar tested a 14 hp model, and found the vehicle a "good looking, comfortable car of medium size which proves interesting to drive." It was clocked at nearly seventy miles an hour, and

A very early Flying Twenty, obviously one of the first off the line.

Miss Pauline Gower, a pilot with the British Empire Air Display Team, proudly standing with her Flying Sixteen.

returned a creditable 26 mpg.

A large number of Standard chassis was exported to Australia to be bodied over there by local coachbuilding concerns, although a number of complete cars were also sent down under. In July 1937, Prince Chichibu, the brother of the Japanese Emperor, visited the Canley factory, spending a lot of time there, and being chauffeured around the local area in a V-8 Standard.

SS Cars continued their close relationship with the Company, although by the time that 1937 was drawing to a close, Avon had decided to cease volume production. For years, the firm had been run by

John Maudslay, Reginald's son, on very special financial terms. It was this part that Black objected to, as Standard often did not get paid until the Avon car was sold. Black made an offer to take over the coachbuilder, but instead, Maudslay liquidated the company, and all links were severed there and then. Avon continued to trade in one form or another, however, until very recently, moving to nearby Leamington Spa.

At least the Shadow Factory Scheme was

Avon were still very active so far as Standard were concerned. This is a 1936 Avon Flying Twenty.

Mr and Mrs Maudslay of Avon with their 1936 Flying Twenty drophead coupé.

An elegant Avon Flying Twenty saloon dating from late in 1936.

This Police car bodied by Avon was also based on the Flying Twenty chassis.

Slightly later than AWD 222, this superb Avon Flying Sixteen survives, and can often be seen on the road today en route to classic car events.

going Black's way, and already Bristol aero-engine parts were leaving the new site in preparation for an increasingly likely war. Production figures were also good, with 40,000 vehicles being built in 1937 and totals still rising at an absolutely staggering rate.

About this time the Company was looking at the possibilities of introducing a front-wheel drive car. Little is known of this 6 hp model, but at least one prototype was completed. It had a two-door body, and a rather stubby front end design.

On the 10th of March, 1938, King George VI visited the Shadow Factory at Canley. 4,000 people were now employed by Standard on a 47 hour week basis, and sales were still consistently reaching new records.

The 1938 models were basically the same as those marketed in the previous year, but all now featured the new waterfall-style grille as seen on the V-8, and modified lighting arrangements. The shell of the radiator and its centre bar were finished in body colour, to further help distinguish the cars from 1937 models, and extra sound insulation was added.

Later in March, the Flying Twelve Super Saloon and Drophead Coupé were introduced, followed in July by the Flying Fourteen Super Saloon, and the Flying Twenty Super Saloon, all with central chassis lubrication, enhanced trim and fittings, and slightly modified bodies.

October saw the introduction of the Flying Eight in saloon, De Luxe and tourer forms, all of which carried an independent front suspension. Each had the same 1,021cc four-cylinder engine, and their prices were £129, £139, and £125 respectively.

From this date onwards, the Flying Ten Super and the Flying Twelve Super were also made available with this improved suspension set up. The famous bodymakers, Fisher & Ludlow, managed to land the contract to supply the bodies for the new small Standard, and so erected a purpose-built factory in the Tile Hill area of Coventry for this operation. Nowadays, of course, it is used by Peugeot-Talbot for stores.

By 1939, the Fourteen and Twenty models had gained the option of independent front suspension, and in January, the Super Nine and Popular Nine were introduced, later to be joined by a drophead coupé version of the Standard Eight.

Save for the debut of a four-door Eight, the 1940 model year cars would have remained much the same had they been produced in any reasonable numbers, but sadly, other events took priority. Captain Black took delivery of a superb Mulliner-bodied limousine on the SS Jaguar 3.5 litre chassis just as the bad news broke.

On the 3rd of September 1939, Britain declared war on Nazi Germany. The First World War had been horrific, but nobody could have been prepared for the mass destruction that followed over the next six years. By necessity, car manufacturers turned their attentions to the production of military equipment of one sort or another, be it fighting vehicles, guns or aircraft.

Chapter Nine looks in detail at what the Standard Motor Company did towards the Allied effort during the Second World War ...

The 1937 two-door Flying Nine. It sold for just £149.

Alick Dick putting one of the pool cars through its paces at one of the local Standard gatherings, late in 1937.

The V8 saloon, first shown to the public at the 1936 Olympia Motor Show. There was also a rare dhc version.

The interior of a Flying Light Twelve. The design would stay virtually the same until the outbreak of the Second World War.

An Avon Flying Twelve drophead coupé from 1936.

A 1937 Flying Fourteen pictured in Broadway, a village in Hereford & Worcestershire, and close to the Company test route.

A proud moment as the 30,000th Flying Twelve rolls off the production line. John Black is seen standing third from the right.

The Australian version of the Flying Twelve drophead coupé, known as the Roadster.

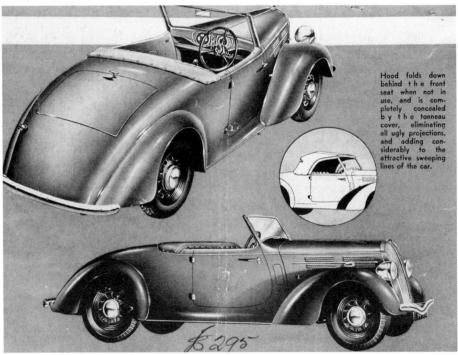

Hood folds down behind the front seat when not in use, and is completely concealed by the tonneau cover, eliminating all ugly projections, and adding considerably to the attractive sweeping lines of the car.

Flying Standard "TWELVE"

The Standard Flying Twelve in profile.

An Avon-bodied 1938 Flying Fourteen Super dhc. The factory later copied the design.

The Flying Nine from the same period.

The 1938 model Flying Twelve, distinguished by its grille finished in body colour.

The Touring Saloon version of the Flying Fourteen.

The two-door Flying Eight, some 10,000 of which were built pre-war.

A newly-restored 1938 two-door Flying Nine...

One of the rare four-door Flying Eight saloons.

And a touring version of the Flying Eight.

IX: PRODUCTION FOR VICTORY

During the very early part of the War, the Company still managed to produce the odd Flying Eight saloon for private use, as well as a few Nine, Ten, Twelve and Fourteen models.

Hundreds of 10, 12 and 14 hp chassis were fitted with pick-up or utility van bodies, and some were even converted later on to become ambulances. Quite a few of the smaller 8 hp versions were equipped with box bodies and used as YMCA tea dispensers! However, as the so-called phoney war turned into something very real, production moved over wholly to war work.

The Shadow Factory Scheme was undoubtedly what saved this country from suffering defeat in the Second World War. The Standard Motor Company was involved in the project from its birth until the day when, thankfully, it was no longer needed.

With the new threat to peace in Europe posed by the Nazi Party, new legislation was passed in order to arm the country in case of war. The Shadow Factory Scheme, as it was called, proposed that certain companies should be paid by the Government to run extra sites devoted purely to the manufacture of weapons, aircraft, engines, and other such necessities.

A number of Coventry-based concerns were involved in the Scheme, notably Standard, Daimler, Rover, the Rootes Group, and the famous engineering company, Alfred Herbert. In all of these cases, either new works or extensions were paid for by the Government, who over-viewed production, but left the management side of things to the individual firms.

Mosquito fuselage assembly at the new Ansty site.

Late in 1936, work began on a £650,000 aircraft factory, built on the site of the old works golf course. Within just four years, the first of the new "Flying Standards" had made its debut; an Oxford Trainer. The Airspeed AS.10 Oxford I was powered by two Armstrong-Siddeley Cheetah radial engines, and first went into service with the R.A.F. in the January of 1938. By the time the Oxford had been withdrawn, 4,411 examples had been built, and of those, 750 were constructed by the Standard Company.

By far the most famous Standard-built aircraft, however, was the de Havilland Mosquito. The Mosquito, affectionately known as the "Wooden Wonder", was originally conceived in 1938 as a fast, small bomber.

Standard-built Mosquito aircraft on a snow-bound British airfield.

Above: the rather primitive-looking Beaverette Mk.I, based on the 14 hp chassis. The Beaverette name was chosen to honour of Lord Beaverbrook - the Minister of Aircraft Production.

Right: a rear view of the Mk.IV Beaverette, and below, the same vehicle from the side. It was used by the R.A.F. to protect their airfields, and by the Home Guard.

The first Oxford I fuselage built at the Canley works, early 1941. The Standard works were very lucky during the Blitz, escaping most of the bombing.

It was to have the speed of a fighter aircraft, a 1,500 mile range, and the capacity to carry a 1,000 lb bomb load. The first one flew in November 1940, powered by two of the legendary Rolls-Royce Merlin engines.

There were nearly thirty types of Mosquito, but the one built by Standard was the FB.VI; a fighter-bomber developed from the Mk.II aircraft. It had the usual equipment associated with a fighter, but also accommodation for two 500 lb bombs. Further bombs, drop-tanks or rocket launchers could be fitted under the wings, making this a truly potent machine. These aircraft saw action with Coastal Command, as well as over Europe and Burma.

Bristol "Mercury VIII" aero-engines were also built in the Banner Lane Shadow Factory, and these had started to find their way to the R.A.F. by mid-1937. By the end of the conflict, around 20,000 of them had been produced, in addition to the many

other aero-engine components, totalling nearly half-a-million units. These included carburettors, cylinders, and constant speed devices.

Around 3,000 Bristol Beaufighter fuselages were also constructed, along with roughly 250,000 bomb release slips. As if this wasn't enough, the Company produced over 10,000 vehicles (vans, utilities and ambulances) for the effort, 5,000 Gwynne fire pumps, and a range of light armoured cars.

The Beaverette Light Armoured Car was introduced on the 14 hp chassis, and the Mk.I model was quickly followed by the Mk.II, III and IV versions, each carrying varying amounts of armour and weaponry.

The Beaverette range was frankly a little antiquated in its design, using steel plates backed up by oak planks for armour on an almost standard chassis. By the time that the Mk.III was introduced, a shorter wheelbase was used, and it at least looked a little less

The Mosquito Shop at Ansty, just outside Coventry.

The Jungle Bug. At least two examples are known to survive.

One of the many trucks built by the Company for the Allied war effort.

like something out of a *Dad's Army* sketch.

However, Beaverettes were only supposed to be Light Armoured Cars, mainly for use by the Home Guard and, in that respect, served their purpose admirably. In all, around 4,000 armoured cars were built.

Utility production continued throughout the war, mainly on the 12 hp and 14 hp chassis, although there were at least two interesting projects carried out during 1943 and 1944 respectively. The first was a 12 hp cross-country vehicle, similar to the Willys Jeep, though this was never put into production.

The machine dating from 1944 was christened the "Jungle Bug", and with its modified 8 hp engine, it was intended for use in airborne operations. The first prototype had conventional two-wheel drive, but the second version was fitted with four-wheel drive. Capable of around thirty miles per hour, the Jungle Bug was supposed to be capable of being dropped from an aeroplane along with a small trailer, and traversing all sorts of terrain including rivers and lakes. The latter requirement was its downfall, as it failed miserably in the watersports category. Whilst the design team was contemplating how to stop the machine sinking at every opportunity, the Jeep was successfully adapted for airborne missions, and the project was cancelled before the Jungle Bug was ever perfected.

In the September of 1945, the Second World War finally came to an end after six long years of fighting. It had left virtually every country in Europe completely devastated, and it would be a long time before any sort of normality returned to the world.

The incredible commitment shown by the Standard Motor Company was fairly typical of all those involved in the Shadow Factory Scheme, but this does not take anything away from its achievements. In fact, for this and his services on the Joint Aero-Engine Committee, Captain J. P. Black was knighted.

A 1941 14 hp Utility that has survived for over fifty years.

Aircraft built by the Standard Motor Company during World War Two

Serial No.	Aircraft	Qty	Notes
V3865 - 3914 V3933 - 3957 V3972 - 3996 V4016 - 4065 V4079 - 4103 V4124 - 4173 V4192 - 4241 V4259 - 4283	Airspeed AS.10 Oxford I	300	Built for the R.A.F. (Feb 1941 onwards)
DF220 - 264 DF276 - 314 DF327 - 367 DF390 - 433 DF445 - 489 DF501 - 536	Airspeed AS.10 Oxford I	250	Built for the R.A.F.
HP848 - 888 HP904 - 942 HP967 - 989 HR113 - 162 HR175 - 220 HR236 - 262 HR279 - 312 HR331 - 375 HR387 - 415 HR432 - 465 HR485 - 527 HR539 - 580 HR603 - 648	DH.98 Mosquito FB.VI	500	Built for the R.A.F. (June 1943 - Dec 1944)
LB401 - 429 LB442 - 462	Airspeed AS.10 Oxford I	50	Built for the R.A.F.
MP275 - 314 MP338 - 376 MP391 - 430 MP444 - 474	Airspeed AS.10 Oxford I	150	Built for the R.A.F.
RF580 - 625 RF639 - 681 RF695 - 736 RF749 - 793 RF818 - 859 RF873 - 915 RF928 - 966	DH. 98 Mosquito FB.VI	300	Built for the R.A.F. (Dec 1944 - June 1945)
TE587 - 628 TE640 - 669 TE683 - 707 TE708 - 725	DH. 98 Mosquito FB.VI	115	Built for the R.A.F. and the Royal Navy. (May 1945 - Dec 1945)
TE738 - 780 TE793 - 830 TE848 - 889 TE905 - 932	DH. 98 Mosquito FB.VI	151	Built for the R.A.F. (May 1945 - Dec 1945)
TE933 - 944 TE958 - 999	DH. 98 Mosquito FB.VI	53	Order cancelled.

*HP 848 - the very first Mosquito built by the Standard Motor Co. It
was completed in June 1943.*

The 1066th and last Mosquito built by Standard, seen here with the postwar range of motor cars.

X: THE IMMEDIATE POSTWAR YEARS

Sensing the end of the War, Standard announced that the Eight and Twelve were to be quickly put back into production once the hostilities ceased - this was in May 1945. Four months after their Press Release, peace returned to the world, and sure enough, the pre-war models were soon back on the line.

The speed with which the Company returned to full production was quite staggering. However, it was later revealed that Black had ordered the tracks *et cetera* to be stored at the Ansty site, and as soon as the War ended, they were once again laid in the Canley works.

The Eight, with its 1,009cc engine, was available as either a two-door saloon or open tourer. It had the benefit of a new four-speed gearbox, as opposed to the old three-speed unit, but otherwise, at least in saloon form, was very much the same as its earlier counterpart. Externally, only the lack of louvres down the side of the bonnet distinguished them.

The Eight Tourer, on the other hand, had a completely new body, even though at a quick glance there was little to tell the pre- and postwar models apart.

The Twelve was also available as a saloon or a tourer (or more correctly, a drophead coupé). The saloon was a six-light four-door machine, capable of carrying five in comfort, whilst the drophead had a two-door body which would happily accommodate

Sir John Black, pictured in the early part of 1952.

four people.

Both Twelve models came with chrome-plated grille surrounds, and the option of a 14 hp engine. The standard 12 hp unit was bored to give 1,609cc, and the extra power was obtained by taking the block out to 1,776cc.

In the words of *The Autocar* magazine, "Although the main features of the postwar models are not a great deal changed, it is evident that careful attention has been paid to refinements which will mean a lot to the eventual owner." The magazine later noted that, "Generally, the finish is rather above that of the present run of postwar cars, but not yet up to the pre-war Standards in small details."

Soon the saloons were being joined by a timber-bodied estate car version of each due to steel being in short supply. To the disgust of enthusiasts, no longer were the cars called "Flying Standards", this title being given only to the true pre-war models.

During the War, frantic negotiations were afoot to obtain the Triumph Motor Company. There is more than a touch of irony about this tale, for it was Siegfried Bettmann, the Chairman of Standard in pre-WWI days, who had founded the Triumph marque.

Bettmann was born in 1863, a German with a Jewish heritage. Just after his twentieth birthday,

Advert for the post-war Standard Eight. The script mentions "Flying" Eight, but this designation was never adopted on postwar models; it was simply an Eight.

A 1946 Standard Twelve saloon, owned by Standard Motor Club member, Les Longley.

Bettmann found himself in London, and quickly moved into the booming bicycle trade. His first machines were built for him in Birmingham, and carried the Triumph name. By 1887, a small factory in Coventry had been acquired, and with his partner, Mauritz Schulte and a number of smaller investors, Bettmann created a company that would become world famous.

As the cycle industry died off, Triumph moved into motorcycles, experimenting before the turn of the century, but going into full production by 1903. It was in this year that Triumph built a tricar, but four-wheeled machines were still a long way off. Meanwhile, the Triumph motorcycle was developed, and Bettmann built up a massive list of useful contacts.

One of those contacts was Reginald Maudslay, founder of the Standard Motor Company. You will recall that Maudslay desperately wanted to regain full control of his company from Sir Charles Friswell, well, one of the people who helped finance this move was none other than Siegfried Bettmann. In return, he was given a seat on the Board, and became Chairman for 1911 and 1912. In the meantime, Bettmann was becoming very involved with politics, and was Lord Mayor of Coventry by the start of the 1914 War.

In 1923, Triumph moved into the motor car business, buying the old Dawson works in Coventry's Priory Street. The first car was a four-cylinder 10/20 hp model and, very quickly, it was joined by a whole range of vehicles.

By far the most important car for Triumph in these early days was the so-called "Super Seven". Powered by an 850cc engine, this model was extremely popular, with over 17,000 being produced

The postwar Standard Eight in profile. Note the lack of bonnet louvres.

The larger postwar drophead coupés on the Twelve and Fourteen chassis were very elegant.

Siegfried Bettmann, 1863 - 1951.
Founder of the Triumph marque, and
once Lord Mayor of Coventry.

The Triumph Super Seven was extremely popular, and launched the
firm into serious car manufacture.

before its run came to an end.

When the mid-thirties arrived, Triumph turned their attention from family cars to sports cars, with Donald Healey providing the technical know-how. A number of superb motor cars followed, including the Gloria-Vitesse, and the legendary Dolomite.

However, all was not as well as it appeared on the surface. The bicycle business had been sold off in 1931 and, in 1936, the car and motorcycle sides separated. Bettmann had actually resigned in 1933, but came out of retirement to run the new Triumph Motorcycle Company. He died in 1951.

The Triumph motor car continued to flourish, with competition success planting the Company firmly in the big league so far as sports car manufacturers were concerned. By June 1939 though, they were in

the hands of the Receivers with massive debts. Thomas W. Ward Limited of Sheffield acquired the firm in 1940, and managed to produce a short-lived 12 hp car. It was Sir John Black who would save the marque, though.

It was a grand marketing ploy. The Triumph name would allow Black to get into the SS-Jaguar market, as the Standard badge was no longer associated with sporting cars. With Jaguar now making the majority of their engines in-house, Black could afford to take them out of the game.

On the 24th of November 1944, a deal for £75,000 was formally concluded whereby the Standard Motor Company became the official owners of the Triumph car manufacturing business. The Triumph Motor Company (1945) Limited was formed as a wholly-owned subsidiary of Standard.

Triumph cars lined up for delivery outside the old Dawson works.

An interesting 4wd agricultural vehicle was produced by the Standard Company during the last few months of 1945. Based on the 8 hp chassis, it was to have a short life, being replaced by the legendary Ferguson tractor in the September of 1946.

The Ferguson project was quite interesting in that it came about due to the great food shortage of the postwar years. In answer to this, production of agricultural machinery became a priority, and Black wanted at least some of this lucrative market.

Harry Ferguson had had dealings with other car companies pre-war, such as Ford of America, and Morris of England. He was a fine inventor, improving his products at every opportunity.

The first Ferguson tractor came in 1933, built in Belfast. As time went by, an agreement was struck whereby David Brown of Huddersfield (later linked with Aston Martin of course), would build the ma-chines, and Harry Ferguson would sell them.

Ferguson and Brown parted company just before the outbreak of the Second World War, and Ferguson went back to Henry Ford with his new ideas. However, because Ford in the States and the British Ford were separate entities, after the War, Ferguson was free to choose who he wanted to deal with in the UK.

Ferguson and the Chairman of Ford UK, Lord Perry, did not get on very well, and so Sir John Black of the Standard Motor Company was approached. Black was very receptive, due to the reasons outlined earlier, and the Banner Lane factory was allocated to tractor production, the first examples leaving there late in 1946.

The 8, 12, and 14 hp cars were continued for 1946 and the early part of 1947, although they were now joined by a Triumph 1800 in both roadster and

Lord Leigh and his rather attractive Triumph Gloria-Vitesse.

Donald Healey (far right), helped to build up Triumph's reputation for fine sports cars - a reputation that has lasted to this day.

saloon guises. This latest model made use of the engines that were now surplus to Jaguar's requirements, as they now made their own 2.5 and 3.5 litre units, using Standard for just the smaller 1.8 litre engine.

Raymond Mays, the driving force behind such projects as ERA, and the Raymond Mays Specials based on the Standard V-8 chassis, approached Sir John Black with his ideas for BRM - British Racing Motors. Black promised help in a number of ways. Not only did he donate £5,000 on behalf of the Company, but he also promised his team would design and build a Test House at Bourne. Engine components for the 1.5 litre V-16 were also built by Standard, but at the end of the day, Mays was just far too ambitious. The V-16 was a dismal failure. Fortunately, in later years, BRM would save face and win a number of Grands Prix, but with much simpler machines.

Sir John was looking at simplifying the Standard range. He knew that to stay strong, the foreign markets were as, if not more important, to the future of the Company than the home market.

Early postwar British cars had blotted their copy book somewhat abroad, as their designs were basically too old to cope with modern demands.

Black decided to pin all his hopes on one vehicle, a new car that would use proven technology, a modified tractor engine, and be suitable for both the home and, perhaps more importantly, overseas markets. It was a massive gamble, for if the public didn't like the car, the Company would have nothing else to sell in its place. However, July 1947 saw the introduction of what must surely be classed as Standard's most important model ever - the Vanguard. The next chapter looks at Britain's first all-new postwar car.

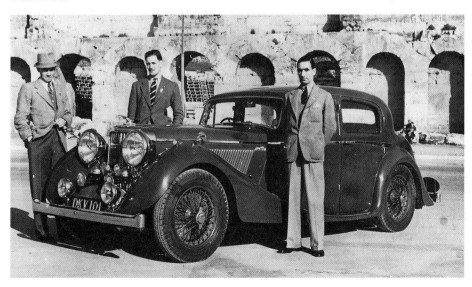

A 3.5 litre Jaguar saloon in Athens, ready for the start of the 1939 Monte Carlo Rally.

Woody estate cars were very common postwar; due to the lack of sheet steel; tax was reduced on these vehicles when buying new. The bodies were built by Mulliners for Standard.

A superb example of the 1946 Standard Eight Tourer.

Notes on chassis (commission) numbers

The commission numbers listed below give a good indication of production per year, as the commencement figure corresponds to the month and year shown on the left.

Eights

July 1945	NA 1
January 1946	NA 1711
January 1947	NA 19344
January 1948	NA 42063

Common prefixes and suffixes -

DL -	Saloon	T4 - Tourer
SC -	Estate	
CP -	Drophead Coupé	
CO -	Chassis Only	

Twelves

July 1945	DD 1
January 1946	DD 490
January 1947	DD 4107
January 1948	DD 7828
July 1948	DD 8548

Fourteens

January 1946	ED 265
January 1947	ED 5993
January 1948	ED 13735
July 1948	ED 15085

XI: VANGUARD - THE EXPORT DRIVE

Still suffering from a lack of suitable materials, motor manufacturers were forced into exporting as many vehicles as possible, even if it meant disappointing dealers on the home market. As mentioned earlier, very few British car producers had new designs, so were basically building pre-war machines to meet the massive demand.

The Standard Vanguard, styled by the ex-Triumph man Walter Belgrove, and engineered by Harry Webster and Ted Grinham, was Great Britain's first all-new postwar car. Announced to the public on the 18th of July 1947, it had many novel features which would act as a guide for the rest of the industry.

Introduced with a four-cylinder 1,850cc ohv engine, the production models were bored out to 2,088cc, giving the car around 68 bhp. With a three-speed transmission, and column change (the latter, undoubtedly to suit the American market), the Vanguard was easily capable of seventy-five miles an hour, whilst returning about 26 mpg.

The all-steel bodywork was designed to carry five people in comfort, and was very modern-looking. Again it was probably designed to appeal just as much to American eyes, as the more traditional British enthusiasts. Indeed, Sir John had sent Belgrove to the US Embassy in London to sketch the latest American cars.

Despite the UK's steel shortage the efforts made by the Company during the War ensured enough was made available to enable Standard to produce between one and two thousand Vanguards a week over the following months, the vast majority of the cars going abroad.

In October 1948, the Vanguard saloon was joined by an estate car version, a 12cwt van and a pick-up truck. Shortly afterwards, the Triumph Roadster and saloon gained the larger 2.1 litre Vanguard engine, and on the small car side of the Standard business, there had already been major changes.

The last of the old style Standard Eights had been discontinued in the July of 1948, whilst the Twelve and Fourteen models followed not long after, the final cars rolling off the line long before the Motor Show.

On the first day of December 1948, Mr C. J. Band presided (as Chairman), over the 45th Annual General Meeting of the Standard Motor Company. It was noted by both Band and Black that there was still a distinct lack of steel, but the Company had still made a good profit, even after the massive investment made in machinery. The most important news though concerned the appointment of Alick Dick to the position of Assistant Managing Director.

Dick was born in Norfolk in 1916, and received his education in Cheltenham. He had joined Standard in 1934 as an apprentice, but quickly moved up the ladder to become Sir John Black's P.A., then a Director of the Company. Although his incredible rise to the top could have been explained by Dick being a distant relation of Black's, it was in fact so

Sir John Black with his new baby, the Vanguard.

Phase I Vanguard fascia.

distant, it would have had little or no bearing on events. He was simply very good at his job, and he would continue to have an increasingly important role to play in the Company's fortunes.

Black was given a tax free gift of Company shares in 1949, but Sir Stafford Cripps brought in new legislation to ensure that he was taxed. In the end, the gift was virtually worthless. Ironically, Cripps was a socialist, and it was Black who had made the Standard workers some of the best paid men in Coventry.

By this time, of course, all Standard car production was devoted towards the Vanguard, although the Triumph Roadster and saloon (now known as the Renown), continued to be built alongside them. Another Triumph was to appear just in time for the 1950 trading season, but we shall look at the Standard-built Triumphs in detail in a later chapter.

The Vanguard was still selling well, with many going to the various British Ministries, as well as VIPs such as HRH the Duke of Gloucester, Earl Mountbatten of Burma and Lord Brabazon, to name but a few.

In 1950, three Vanguards were entered in the Monte Carlo Rally. One of the cars was driven by Tommy Wisdom and Norman Black and, although none of them featured in the results - the event was won by Becquart and Secret in a Hotchkiss - the Company could take some consolation in the fact that only five of the 308 starters actually finished without losing time.

By May 1950, Tickfords was offering a full roll-top roof for the Vanguard, and in the following month, overdrive became an option for the popular model, as it did on the Renown, which by now was fitted with independent front suspension.

Midway through 1951, the Company was approached by Rolls-Royce with a view to producing R-R Avon aero-engines. These turbo-jets were to power the English Electric "Canberra" - a fine bomber aircraft used by the R.A.F. Between 1952 and 1955, over four hundred were built.

Negotiations also took place between Sir John and George Mason of the Nash Corporation concerning the possibilities of Standard building the NX1. However, the deal fell through, and Austin eventually went on to build the machine, known by then as the Metropolitan.

An Extraordinary General Meeting was held during June of '51, and the Company's nominal capital was increased from £2m to a staggering £6m. Alick Dick was appointed the Deputy Managing Director, and negotiations were opened up concerning the possibility of building another factory near Liverpool. It was noted shortly afterwards that the 200,000th Ferguson tractor had just been completed.

The Vanguard was given a revised radiator grille in time for the 1951 Motor Show, as well as a slightly wider back window. This new model became known as the Phase IA. Very little changed on the Vanguard then until the March of 1953, when the Phase II featuring a restyled boot was introduced to compliment the other features of the car. During the early part of 1953, negotiations took place between

An unusual shot of the Phase I Vanguard, taken for publicity purposes.

the Standard Company and Willys-Overland of North America. The Company were trying to gain the rights to build the Jeep in Coventry, and in return, Willys would market Standards in the USA. Sadly, nothing came of the idea, despite the detailed plans drawn up on both sides of the Atlantic.

However, despite this drawback with an American distributor, associated companies were formed in Australia, India, Canada and South Africa. Sir John Black was the Chairman of each concern, which at first assembled Standard cars and, in some cases, manufactured them. Markets would be secured in other countries as well in the near future, such as Belgium, Switzerland, Eire, New Zealand, Sweden and Denmark.

Ferguson tractors had been steadily produced in large numbers since 1946 in both petrol- and diesel-engined form, but in the September of '53, Harry Ferguson Limited merged with Massey-Harris, eventually going on to form a new concern called Massey-Ferguson. The famous Massey-Ferguson tractor continues in production at Banner Lane to this day, and is still one of the most respected manufactur-

The Vanguard was tested to its limits before being put on sale to the public.

A beautifully-restored example of the Phase I Standard Vanguard. The name Vanguard, incidently, came from the British ship, first launched in 1586, and the bodies were built at Fisher & Ludlow.

ers of agricultural machinery in the world.

Other goings-on in 1953 included the introduction of the 803cc Standard Eight - a new small and functional car which will be described in the next chapter, along with the Standard Ten which made its debut in the following year in several different forms.

A number of engines were ordered by Morgan for their sports cars, and December saw the launch of the new Swallow Doretti. Based on the TR2, and built by the Swallow Coachbuilding Company of Walsall, it received a lot of attention from the Standard management, and may even have gone on to have been a Standard-Triumph production model had it not have been for an unfortunate accident involving Sir John Black and the works test driver, Ken Richardson ...

At the 1953 AGM, Black was invited to be Chairman in succession to C. J. Band, who had held this office in an unbroken run since 1934. However, Black was forced to retire by January 1954, supposedly because of ill health brought about by the accident in the Doretti. A Press Release was issued later that month -

"The Standard Motor Company Limited regretfully announces that Sir John Black has found it necessary to relinquish his offices of Chairman and Managing Director and his membership of the Board of Directors of the Company.

"It will be recalled that Sir John Black was involved in a most unfortunate motor car accident last November in which he sustained considerable personal injuries, and after consultation with his medical adviser, his wife and close friends, he has been advised to take this action ."

This release was obviously a smoke-screen to cover up the Board's discontent with Black's managerial tactics, brought to a head after the works Christmas Party when Black decided to sack a number of his management team, including E. G. Grinham.

In fact, it was Alick Dick's wife who had typed out Black's resignation letter, which he simply had to sign. It ended -

"It is with the greatest regret that I have

The headlight alignment area at Canley. Vanguard saloons, estates and vans can be seen in the picture.

reluctantly come to this decision, and I wish my efficient team every success in carrying on where I left off."

In the end, Black was given a golden handshake, Lord Tedder took his place, Alick Dick became the Managing Director, and E. G. Grinham the Deputy.

Much of the competition history during this period involved either Standard Tens or Triumph sports cars, the Vanguard keeping something of a low profile. However, the Stoddart brothers campaigned their Vanguard in the 1954 Monte Carlo Rally, starting from Glasgow.

In the meantime, Alick Dick had virtually completed a deal with Rover regarding a merger. However, Rover's Finance Director stopped it at the last minute.

The first of the diesel-engined Vanguards were released in the August of 1954. Although very few were ever sold, the old Ferguson power-unit was made available in the Vanguard saloons, pick-ups, estates and vans.

Sir John may have been controversial, but his brilliant gamble had obviously paid off. The decisions to concentrate on the Vanguard, along with Ferguson tractors and Triumph models, were amongst the most important made in the history of the Company.

At the 1955 Motor Show, the third in the series of Vanguards was introduced; the Phase III. After looking at the smaller Eights and Tens, the next chapter reviews the history of the Phase III Vanguard.

A Phase I pick-up with a rather agricultural-looking rear cover. These were built for HM Forces.

Another Phase I, this time a prototype taxi dating from 1949. It has a division and two occasional seats, with the taxi sign being situated above the front screen.

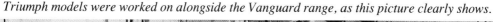

Triumph models were worked on alongside the Vanguard range, as this picture clearly shows.

Above: One of the earliest Vanguards from 1947, photographed next to the contemporary HMS Vanguard.

Right: The Vanguard Phase IA seen from the rear. Introduced in time for the 1951 Motor Show, the wider rear window is very evident.

Below: The new grille arrangement of the Phase IA models.

An early example of the Phase IA estate, which are now a very rare sight.

The Imperia works in Belgium, pictured during the mid-fifties when Standards were built there.

The Vanguard Phase II was a more conventional three-box saloon, available from 1953 to 1955.

The Stoddart brothers driving their Vanguard on the 1954 Monte Carlo Rally.

The Vanguard, seen here as a restored pick-up at a Standard Motor Club rally.

Notes on the Phase I and II chassis (commission) numbers

The following information shows the chassis number commencing at the start of the month noted on the left. This gives a good indication of production figures month by month.

Phase I

April 1948	V 1
July 1948	V 188
October 1948	V 1747
January 1949	V 7907
July 1949	V 29991
September 1949	V 37730
January 1950	V 52001
July 1950	V 80275
October 1950	V 94000
January 1951	V 108145
July 1951	V 133249
October 1951	V 150000
January 1952	V 154337
July 1952	V 172246
October 1952	V 178673

Final chassis:
January 1953   V 184799 DL

Phase II

October 1952	V200001
January 1953	V200350
July 1953	V215993
January 1954	V232580
February 1954	V 233380
July 1954	V 246390
September 1954	V 250738
January 1955	V 261278
July 1955	V 273879

Final chassis:
August 1955	V 276222 DL
July 1956	V 281074 SC
April 1958	V 286070 V

Phase II Diesel

March 1954	DEC 1
September 1954	DEC 463

Final chassis:
September 1955   DEC 1754

Common suffixes to Phase I and Phase II cars -

DL or DLO	Saloon
V	Van
SC or SW	Estate
PU	Pick-up

Left-hand drive cars had an L in front of the suffixes listed above.

Mark Denton's superb 1952 Vanguard in suitably majestic surroundings.

XII: EIGHTS & TENS

Because of the importance of the Eights and Tens to the development of the Standard Company, they have been given their own chapter so as not to be overshadowed by the larger Vanguards and more glamorous Triumph sports cars of the time.

The 8 hp Standard Eight, so nearly christened the Beaver, was introduced in 1953 - a very spartan, basic little car with an 803cc four-cylinder engine. Even such things as a second windscreen wiper blade, a heater and nave plates were optional, and there was an absolute minimum of trim.

In retrospect, it is easy to criticise and say it is obvious why the car was not a hit with the British public - it was just too basic, even at £481. However, look at the success of the Citroen 2CV, or the Volkswagen Beetle, and Ted Grinham can be excused for going along this route. The saving grace was the power unit, able to take the car up to just over sixty miles an hour, whilst still returning between forty and fifty miles to the gallon. For the following year, the interior was upgraded, and the Eight became an immediate success.

In May 1954, the Ten was released with an enlarged 948cc engine, fully trimmed bodyshell and winding windows. This same body was used for the new Eight De Luxe mentioned earlier, which came out in the same month. Prices were set at £538 for the

Eight De Luxe, and £580 for the Ten.

Of the Ten, *The Autocar* noted that "the Standard Ten is a very practical car for the family man. In the design, first things have been put first, so that performance and road holding are very satisfactory."

June spawned the Ten estate (known as the Companion), as well as a 6cwt van and 6cwt pick-up based on the Ten. Flashing indicators, first seen on the Beauvais-styled 1933 Avon Coupé, were by now fitted to all of the Eights and Tens.

During May of 1955, the so-called Family Eight replaced the basic model, selling at £509. One was driven non-stop around Britain (a total of 1,916 miles), in under forty-seven hours, proving the car's potential. Furthermore, Jimmy Ray drove a Ten to victory on the 1955 RAC Rally, with Ken Richardson bringing a similar car home in third place. Maurice Gatsonides took fourth on the Tulip Rally, again in a Standard Ten.

At the Motor Show in October 1955, the Super Eight and Super Ten made their debut, with enhanced trim and equipment. These Super models replaced the De Luxe cars, and were joined, in March 1956 by the basic Family Ten. This gave a range consisting of the Family Eight, Super Eight, Family Ten, and the Super Ten.

Later on in the year, the two-pedal "Standrive"

The basic Standard Eight was introduced in September 1953, and ran until the May of 1955. A car similar to the Renault 4CV was considered initially, to compete with the Ford Popular.

system was made available on the smaller Standard models, such as the Super Ten Phase II and, again, competition success was achieved with class wins for the Standard Ten in the 1956 RAC Rally, and the Team Prize in the Tulip Rally of the same year with three works Standard Eights driven by Wallwork and Bleakley, Hopkirk and Garvey, and O'Mara-Taylor and Tracey.

The Family Eight Phase II appeared just before the end of the year, and had a much-improved interior, bringing good reports from the car magazine testers.

1957, and the Eights and Tens were now available in Gold Star form, with increased power and modified radiator grilles. These models were given the option of overdrive, as well as a boot which could be opened from the outside on the Eights - progress! The Pennant, a restyled Ten, was introduced later on in the year. It was equipped to a higher standard than its cheaper stablemates, and was finished in any number of bright colour schemes. Otherwise, the range was kept very much the same until the small cars were killed off.

However, the Ten and Pennant models were still campaigned with a certain amount of success. The 1958 Monte Carlo Rally saw Cyril Corbishley take second in Class in his Ten, and John Wallwork in a similar car did equally well. The RAC Rally Team Prize went to the three Pennants entered by the Company, as well as the first three places in the up to 1,300cc Class, and Gatsonides was second in his Class on the Tulip Rally.

The Eight, Ten, and Pennant were all discontinued during 1960, when production of the Triumph Herald was stepped up. However, the Companion did continue for a little while longer, albeit with a Pennant-style front end, introduced in April of 1959.

The Standard Ten Super. It was produced for one year from October 1955.

The production line at Canley during the mid-fifties. Vanguards were built alongside Eights and Tens.

Summary of Eight and Ten production

Eight (basic)	9/53 - 5/55	Family Ten	2/56 - 4/57
Eight De Luxe	5/54 - 10/55	Super Ten Ph.II	10/56 - 10/57
Family Eight	5/55 - 12/56	Ten Gold Star	4/57 - 7/59
Super Eight	10/55 - 2/57	Pennant	10/57 - 5/59
Family Eight Ph.II	12/56 - 4/57	Companion	6/55 - 4/57
Eight Gold Star	4/57 - 7/59	Super Companion	10/55 - 10/56
		Family Companion	5/56 - 3/57
Ten	5/54 - 10/55	Super Companion Ph.II	10/56 - 10/57
Super Ten	10/55 - 10/56	Companion Gold Star	10/57 - 4/62

Prefixes
CS - Eight.   BE - Ten, and all Ten-based models except the Pennant. PN - Pennant.
Suffixes
DL - Saloon. DX - De Luxe or Super Eight. DXB - Family Ten. SC - Companion.
SCF - Family Companion. PU - Pick-up. V - Van.

Left-hand drive models had an L placed in front of the suffix.

A basic 1953 Eight ...

... retouched to become a later Family model.

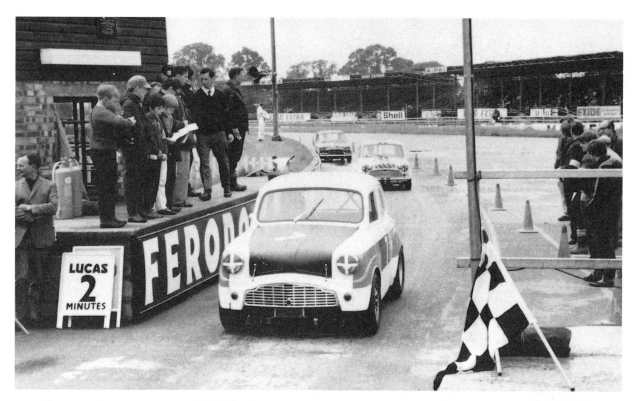

Above: Richard Sandilands campaigned this Standard Eight after an horrific crash in the earlier model shown to the right. Even Stirling Moss, without doubt our finest ever racing driver, had a Standard Eight (with a Ten engine fitted for extra pace). The works also donated a Vanguard van in the mid-fifties, when Moss was running Cooper cars. By 1958, he had moved to a Pennant.

Below: The 1955 RAC Rally team of Tens. The drivers are Jimmy Ray, Bob Dickson, and Ken Richardson.

The Standard Eight Gold Star, this early example dating from April 1957. Both the Gold Star models ran from April '57 to July 1959.

The exclusive car of the year

Exciting new body lines with wide choice of two-tone colour schemes.

Luxurious interior fittings including the new self-breathing Vynair upholstery.

Sports car-type remote control, floor mounted gear lever.

Super power Gold Star engine of 948 c.c. giving 42/47 m.p.g.

Standrive Two-Pedal Control and Laycock Overdrive available as optional extras

The New Standard | PENNANT

Price: £485 Plus P.T. £243.17.0

Advertising for the 1957 Pennant. It was built in saloon form from October 1957 to May 1959.

Bagington Airfield, 1956. The Suez Crisis caused stock piles of Eights, Tens and Companions.

THE **STANDARD** EIGHT

Advertising for the 1957 Eight. Bodies were built by Fisher & Ludlow.

The Standard Ten was badged as the Triumph Ten Sedan for America.

The Standard Ten Dormobile - ideal for weekend trips and family picnics.

For America, the Companion became the Triumph Ten Estate Wagon.

Later Companions had Pennant-style front ends. The last one was built in 1962.

Notes on Eight and Ten chassis (commission) numbers

The chassis numbers shown are those commencing at the start of the month noted on the left.

Eights		Tens	
September 1953	CS 1	May 1954	BE 1
January 1954	CS 9895	September 1954	BE 2675
May 1954	CS 23000	January 1955	BE 11970
September 1954	CS 37610	June 1955	BE 29160
January 1955	CS 50215	September 1955	BE 41300
October 1955	CS 74500	January 1956	BE 53365
January 1956	CS 83100	October 1956	BE 77280
January 1957	CS 86080	January 1957	BE 81000
October 1957	CS 94280	April 1957	BE100000
January 1958	CS 100185	October 1957	BE100400
May 1958	CS 102125	January 1958	BE106000
January 1959	CS 135660	January 1959	BE139170
July 1959	CS 136317	January 1960	BE160525

		Final chassis:	
Pennants		January 1961	BE172225 DL
October 1957	PN 1	January 1962	BE 175180 LDL
January 1958	PN 800		
January 1959	PN 35555		
May 1959	PN 37761		

XIII: THE LAST TRUE STANDARDS

98,647 cars, and 70,909 tractors were produced during 1955, a substantial increase of 35,000 units on 1954, and an indication of the continuing success of the Company. However, the Company's future success depended largely on the Vanguard Phase III, launched at the 1955 Motor Show. It featured a unit-construction body, replacing the old and frankly outdated chassis frame. However, the 2,088cc engine was left unchanged, still giving the car a top speed of over eighty miles an hour.

Naturally, the coachwork was redesigned completely, it now looked like a more conventional three-box machine, even though the early proposals submitted by Walter Belgrove closely resembled the Triumph TRX. The interior was also successfully reworked, but Belgrove left the Company shortly afterwards. In the following year, an estate car version was marketed, as well as a "Sportsman" model which featured a slightly detuned Triumph two-litre sports car engine. The Vanguard III also made its competition debut, coming eighth in the Monte Carlo Rally.

Behind the scenes, the Company commissioned a report on the Dennis Brothers business in relation to "the financial aspect of a proposal for a merger." Nothing came of it, but early in 1956, Beans Industries were taken over, giving Standard thirteen acres of land in Tipton.

The 1956 Vanguard Sportsman engine, based on the Triumph TR3 unit.

Perhaps the most interesting event of that year though was the talks held with Chrysler to see if Standard could design a new small car for Europe sharing a common engine with American models. Sadly, once again, little was to materialise.

At the age of 82, Mr C. J. Band decided it was time to retire from the Board of Directors after 36 years of service to the Company, nineteen of which were spent as Chairman.

The Vanguard Phase III as it was first seen on its introduction.

In the meantime, Standard and Massey-Harris-Ferguson were deep in negotiations over a possible merger. The deal would have been based on a share exchange, and by the summer of 1957, terms had been agreed in principle. However, the value of Massey-Harris-Ferguson shares dropped dramatically on the North American stock market and the merger was no longer in the Standard Company's interests, despite MHF owning a substantial block of Standard shares by this time. Talks were then held with the French car giant, Renault - nothing happened as usual. By far the closest the Standard Motor Company came to a merger in this period was also in 1957, but this time involving the Rootes Group.

The Board would have consisted of Sir William Rootes (Chairman), Lord Tedder (Deputy Chairman), Sir Reginald Rootes (Vice-Chairman), Alick Dick and Geoffrey Rootes as Joint-MDs, and five

The Sportsman model was originally intended to be a Triumph, and indeed, the first few cars carried Triumph badging.

other members from each company. After going into great detail, it is amazing that even this deal fell through. The main problem was with Massey-Ferguson who didn't like the idea of Rootes and Standard merging, so instead suggested closer links between Standard and themselves. As we have mentioned earlier though, the Massey-Harris-Ferguson merger relied on share prices - the rest is history.

A slightly cheaper version of the Vanguard, the Ensign, was introduced during 1957. It featured a 1,670cc ohv engine, and a floor-change gearbox, as opposed to the column change found on the other Vanguards.

The Ten and Vanguard had been produced in, or exported to, various countries over the years. It is interesting to note the many name changes used overseas compared to those used on the home market. For instance, the Ten in Australia was known as the Standard Cadet, whilst in the USA it was called the Triumph Sedan (or Estate Wagon in Companion form). The Vanguard was similarly treated, being known in Australia, for example, as the Standard

Spacemaster.

At the 1958 Motor Show, the Michelotti-styled Vanguard Vignale was shown for the first time. Based on the standard Phase III saloon, and available with either a three-speed column change, four-speed floor change or even a Borg Warner automatic gearbox, it came in both saloon and estate form. Distinguishing features included a new radiator, deeper glass areas front and rear, and new rear light clusters. The Ensign was also given the Michelotti treatment, but to a far lesser extent. On its introduction, the Vignale saloon cost £1,043, with the estate priced at £1,157.

Since its introduction way back in 1949, the Triumph Mayflower had continued steadily, and in Australia, a pick-up version was marketed to compliment the Vanguard pick-up that was already being built there. Australia proved to be a very important outlet for the Standard Company.

At the AGM, it was reported that combined production rose from 107,702 units in 1957, to an incredible 147,616 in 1958. The Canley factory was expanded yet again, gaining a new paint and trim shop, as well as another assembly hall, and the Company quickly snapped up the Forward Radiator Company Limited, and the highly-respected Birmingham-based coachbuilders - Mulliners.

An EGM was held during the August of 1959, when all links with Massey-Ferguson were severed. The tractor builders paid £12.5m for the Banner Lane site, allowing the Company to invest in further production facilities.

When talks with Rover over a possible merger failed for a second time (the first occasion being in 1954), the Company was re-organised.

Standard-Triumph International Limited became the holding company, with several subsidiaries attached; these were the Standard Motor Company, Standard-Triumph Group Services Ltd, Standard-Triumph Sales Ltd, the Triumph Motor Company

Another view of the Vanguard Sportsman, this example dating from August 1956.

(1945) Ltd, Beans Industries Ltd, and Mulliners Ltd. So it was then that the Standard Motor Company became little more than a subsidiary of a parent company which it had itself created.

Naturally, 1959 saw the start of the change from Standard to Triumph orientation, helped along by the introduction of the Michelotti-styled Herald. Other cars in the range remained largely unchanged.

The 56th AGM carried some fairly important points, especially in Lord Tedder's speech. He noted that the Fisher & Ludlow factory had been acquired to make up for the loss of Banner Lane, and the land purchased some time ago in Speke, Liverpool, was at last to be put to use. An £11m works was to be constructed for the use of Standard-Triumph (Liverpool) Limited.

The other interesting statement Lord Tedder made was regarding production. He anticipated that car production alone would exceed the combined car/tractor production of the last financial year, but this was very much a case of wishful thinking.

Harold McMillan maintained power in the October 1959 elections on the basis of a reflationary budget, but his trump card was never effective. The British economy was in a mess, and this reflected in new car sales.

For 1960, the Vanguard saloon and estate models continued unchanged, as did the Ensign and the Triumph TR3. September saw the introduction of the Herald convertible, as well as the Atlas Major (with a 1,670cc Ensign power unit), and the Vanguard Six. The latter had a new 1,998cc six-cylinder ohv engine, and coachwork by Vignale.

The Vanguard Six was capable of over ninety miles an hour, and at just £1,021, represented remarkable value for money. However, all of these events were somewhat overshadowed by what had happened in August of that year, the subject of the next chapter.

A Standard Ensign fitted with a Perkins 4/99 diesel engine. Colin Chapman ordered a TR3 unit in one, making quite a car.

The Vanguard estate prepared for the 1957 Motor Show.

The Vanguard Vignale was introduced for the 1958 Motor Show. Michelotti designed the many styling features.

A Standard car destined to be a Triumph - the prototype Herald at the Vignale studios.

Below: The Vanguard Vignale dating from 1958, the year in which Standard approached Bussing Nutzkraftwagen Gmbh of Germany with a view to possible co-operation on commercial vehicle production.

Notes on chassis (commission) numbers

As before, this list shows the chassis numbers commencing on the date to the left.

Vanguard Phase III

October 1955	V 300001
January 1956	V 302055
August 1956	V 314125
October 1956	V 321010
November 1956	V 321909

Final chassis:

October 1957	V 322587

Vanguard Sportsman

August 1956	TDD 1
October 1956	TDD 411
January 1957	TDD 605
October 1957	TDD 825
January 1958	TDD 870

Final chassis:

March 1958	TDD 905

Ensign Mk.I

October 1957	EN 236
January 1958	EN 1560
May 1958	EN 3605
October 1958	EN 10001
January 1959	EN 10577
January 1960	EN 14516

Vanguard Phase III Vignale

October 1958	V 350001
January 1959	V 354120
January 1960	V 367650

Prefixes and suffixes as per earlier Vanguard models.

Opposite: A 1958 Phase III Vanguard.

XIV: THE LEYLAND TAKEOVER

August 1960 will always be remembered as the beginning of the end for the Standard marque, for that is when the Leyland Motors organisation took the Company over. The history of Leyland is an interesting one, starting just after the First World War so far as cars were concerned, but as far back as 1896 with trucks.

The Leyland car was a 7.3 litre luxury machine designed by the awsome team of John Parry Thomas and Reid Railton. Sadly the tax man put an end to the firm's dream, and only eighteen Leyland Eights were built before production ended in 1922.

A merger with Daimler of Coventry was considered, but negotiations failed at an early stage. Instead, Leyland took on the building of the Trojan car from 1922 to 1928 to augment their commercial vehicle production. After World War Two, Donald Stokes gave the industry a view of what was to come, leading the company into buying Albion, and then Scammell. Not satisfied with just the commercial market, he wanted Leyland to expand into cars again. His first port of call, with Sir Henry Spurrier, would be Canley - they wanted the Standard-Triumph business.

The Vanguard Luxury Six, built between 1961 and 1963.

Lord Tedder had retired as Chairman at the end of 1960, taking on the slightly less stressful position of President, so it was Alick Dick who took over the helm. It was Dick who gave the final approval in August 1960 for a £20m takeover. The assets of the Leyland Group now exceeded £100m, and everyone concerned thought that Dick would have a major part to play in its direction.

However, exactly one year later, Dick and six of his other Directors were asked to leave. Share prices fell dramatically as the news broke, but that was it. Stanley Markland took over as MD, with Donald Stokes becoming the Sales Director of Standard-Triumph International Limited. It was a sad end to Alick Dick's glowing career, and one which he didn't deserve.

For 1961, the Vanguard range continued much as it had before, although it was produced in far smaller numbers. A new £2.5m assembly hall was opened at Canley in the March of 1961, but on a sader note, C. J. Band died later on in the same year, just before Christmas.

With the new regime in charge, emphasis was placed on economy and quality. The management structure was streamlined in such a way that Directors knew exactly what was happening on the shop floor, and sales outlets were developed.

June 1962 saw the last new Standard model introduced - the Ensign De Luxe, both in saloon and estate versions. It had the traditional four-cylinder engine bored at 2,138cc, and would happily cruise at eighty-five miles an hour.

The end of May 1963 saw the last Standard roll off the production lines - an Ensign De Luxe, subsequently registered as "2757 KV", and marking the end of an era. The Company kept it for a couple of years, before it was sold to a private buyer in 1966.

Under Leyland, the loss of the Standard name was fairly inevitable. The American market was used

Engine production at Canley. Compare this to the primitive methods shown in chapter 4.

The Vanguard Luxury Six estate, introduced for the 1961 trading season.

The frontage of the Canley site, pictured in the late 1980s.

to seeing Standard Tens badged as Triumph cars, and the Herald was a definite winner on virtually every market. Why should a forward-looking company like Leyland carry an old name whose past glory had been largely forgotten?

So it was then, the Standard name would have to go. It last appeared on a new private car in 1963, and disappeared from the light commercials two years later when the Leyland badge took its place. However, the Triumph marque continued to prosper, and it is the Standard-built and later Triumph machines that we look at in the next chapter.

The 1962 Ensign De Luxe, shown here in estate form.

The Standard Ensign De Luxe saloon - the last model to carry the Standard name in this country.

Notes on chassis (commission) numbers

This is the last batch of Standard chassis numbers. Prefixes and suffixes were the same as the earlier cars.

Vanguard Phase III Vignale

January 1960	V 367650
January 1961	V 400090
Final chassis: August 1961	V 400210

Vanguard Six Vignale

October 1960	W 1
November 1960	W 852
January 1961	W 3240
July 1961	W 6180
August 1961	W 6631
June 1962	W 7896
January 1963	W 9190
Final chassis: May 1963	W 9953

Note: the suffix BG meant automatic.

Ensign Mk.I

November 1960	EN 15448
January 1961	EN 17843
Final chassis:	EN 17862

Ensign Mk.II

September 1960	EN 25001
January 1961	EN 25053
Final chassis: August 1961	EN 26044

Ensign De Luxe

February 1962	EL 3
May 1962	EL 190
January 1963	EL 1582
Final chassis: May 1963	EL 2318

XV: THE TRIUMPH CONNECTION

As noted earlier, the Triumph car business was bought by the Standard Motor Company in 1945. This chapter looks at the Standard-built Triumphs, as well as the post-1963 models, for the Triumph marque was to outlive its saviour.

The first Triumph cars were built to use up the engines no longer required in such large numbers by Jaguar. There was the 1800 Roadster and the 1800 Saloon with razor-edge styling. Both were priced at £927 for the 1946 trading season. At the 1948 Motor Show, it was announced that the Triumph models would now share the Vanguard engine, the Roadster first, with the Saloon following not long after.

The TRX (or Bullet); one of three prototypes produced during 1950.

The splendid Triumph 1800 Roadster, built from 1946 to 1948.

A 1952 Triumph Mayflower saloon.

The interior of the Triumph Mayflower.

A 1952 Triumph Renown saloon, powered by a 2.1 litre four-cylinder engine ...

... and the limousine model. Note the family resemblance to the Mayflower.

For 1950, a new car was introduced, the Mayflower. It was the first car built by the Company without the use of a separate chassis frame, and had a 1.3 litre engine. The two-door body, clearly based on the Triumph Saloon, had been largely the work of Harry Webster.

The Saloon, now known as the Renown, was given a new chassis featuring independent front suspension for 1950, as well as a new braking system, a new steering mechanism, and various cosmetic improvements.

October 1950 saw the introduction of the splen-

The drophead version of the Mayflower. The Mayflower name was chosen by Lady Black.

did streamlined Triumph Roadster, and the drophead coupé version of the Mayflower. Both were unfortunately shortlived, just three of the Roadsters being built, and Mayflower dhc production ceasing before the end of the year. Despite these two projects being classed as commercial failures, total production figures for cars and tractors combined was soon up to around 600 units per day.

Announced at the 1951 Motor Show, the Renown could now be specified as a limousine and, in November 1952, an exciting new two-litre sports car, the TR2, was shown to the public for the first time. It had a 1,991cc engine derived from the Vanguard, but was fitted with twin-carburettors to power the car at speeds in excess of 110 mph. The chassis is said to have been based on the pre-war Standard Nine, but the TR2 was an immediate hit with enthusiasts at just £555 plus Purchase Tax, bringing open sports car motoring to the masses.

In competition, the TR2 excelled. It won the 1954 RAC Rally in the hands of John Wallwork, and put up a good performance in the Mille Miglia and Le Mans 24hr Race. TR2s also won the Team Prize in the Ulster TT Race. During 1955, more success, with a second in the 1955 RAC Rally, and good results at Le Mans and on the Liege-Rome-Liege Rally.

The TR3 came along in 1956, and immediately began showing its winning ways, taking the Team Prize on the Alpine Rally. It later gained disc brakes,

TRIUMPH SEDAN

Standard Tens were badged as Triumph Sedans for the American market. However, on the home market, the Standard name was retained.

On the other hand, under the new regime, the new Standard saloon - the Herald (seen at the foot of the page), was badged as a Triumph from the time of its launch.

making the vehicle even more competitive. Early in 1958, the TR3 was given a slightly wider grille, and from this modification onwards, the model became known as the TR3A.

A TR3 had been fitted with a Sabrina engine in June 1958 and, in a letter to Alick Dick, M. J. Tustin wrote -

"Incidentally, the Sabrina engine installed in the TR3 has been tried out by Harry [Webster] and he nearly frightened himself to death because it was doing quite 100 mph in third gear, and just beginning to find its feet!"

The Spring of 1959 saw the launch of the Triumph Herald - a name borrowed from Alick Dick's favourite sailing boat. Available in either saloon or coupé form, it reverted back to using a separate chassis frame and, to begin with, used the 948cc Standard Ten engine with a single carburettor for the saloon, and twin-carburettors for the sportier coupe. Other cars in the Standard-Triumph range remained basically unchanged for the '59 season.

September 1960 saw the introduction of the long-awaited Herald convertible. A few Michelotti Triumph Italia 2000 sports models were produced in Italy (based on the TR3 chassis), whilst here in England, the Peerless GT was restyled to become the rather shortlived Warwick GT.

During 1960, Triumph had again been successful in competition. TR3s and Heralds took first and second in the Team Prizes on the RAC Rally, and there were good results at Le Mans and in the Tulip Rally.

The Herald S (a cheaper version of the saloon), was introduced in the March of 1961, alongside the Herald 1200, which was distinguished by rubber bumpers and an 1,147cc engine. There was also an Estate announced.

After its long run, in 1961, the TR3 was replaced by the next in the line, the TR4. This had a slightly larger 2,138cc four-cylinder engine, giving 100 bhp. Most of the early production went straight to America but, more importantly, this was the last new Triumph car to be introduced by the old management of the Standard Motor Company - all future cars

were built under Leyland, of course.

Midway through 1962, a smaller derivative of the Vanguard Six engine (of just 1,596cc) was shoehorned into the Herald chassis, and the new car became the Vitesse 6. It was available in saloon and convertible form, with prices starting at just £837.

The Triumph Spitfire made its debut at the 1962 Earls Court Motor Show, powered by a twin-carburettor version of the 1,147cc engine. It was quickly accepted, and soon, orders worth £6m were recorded against it.

For 1963, the Herald was made available with a tuned Spitfire engine, giving a new model known as the Herald 12/50. The Herald 1200 was continued as before, and the Dove GTR4, based on the TR4 and built by Harringtons, was produced briefly during 1963.

The Standard car was no more, but in the autumn of 1963, the Triumph 2000 saloon was introduced, powered by a development of the Vanguard Six engine. The GT6 and Vitesse two-litre models employed the same power unit, as did the 1965 TR4A, with its new independent rear suspension. Meanwhile, development continued on a new front-wheel drive car, the 1300. This was launched in 1966, and soon became available in more powerful TC form.

Leyland at last merged with British Motor Holdings (the old British Motor Corporation post-1966), after fourteen years of negotiations. In 1968, a new company known as British Leyland was formed. This now brought all of the Standard-Triumph concerns together with Austin, Morris, Jaguar, Daimler, Coventry Climax, Riley, and Wolseley; a truly massive group led by none other than Donald Stokes.

The TR5 was a new car in 1968, powered by a 2.5 litre six-cylinder engine equipped with fuel injection, although it was soon superseded by the TR6 with its new body. The Triumph 2000 had also been given a rather elegant new body, and this could also be bought as the 2.5PI with the TR6 engine fitted.

The Triumph Stag, a luxury 2 + 2 sports car powered by a three-litre V-8 engine, made its debut in 1970, although it was the smaller Triumphs that were changing rapidly.

In 1971, the Toledo, with the old 1300 body, replaced the Herald once and for all. It was quickly superseded by the 1500, and the luxury Dolomite followed at the start of 1972. The Dolomite Sprint had a rather unique 2.0 litre engine which propelled the car along in sports car fashion.

British Leyland, however, was plotting the downfall of most of the historic names in its possession. All Triumph fwd cars were scrapped by 1974, the TR6 went in '75, and by 1977, all the six-cylinder saloons and the good-looking Stag had gone.

The Spitfire, with its 1.5 litre engine, continued from 1975 to 1980, by which time, the TR7 had made its debut, and Triumph had been grouped in a specialist band known as Jaguar-Rover-Triumph Limited, and then promptly taken back out of it.

Amidst all this uncertainty, talks between British Leyland and Honda of Japan were going on in the

The Herald production line at Canley, circa 1960. A separate chassis was used to make Complete Knock Down easier.

An early Vitesse, easily distinguished from the Herald by the twin headlights.

A 1970 model year Triumph Spitfire.

91

The launch of the TR3 at Earls Court, 1956.

background. Negotiations started in 1979 and, as all future large saloon models were to be badged as Rovers, the Triumph badge was allocated for the new hybrid car.

Appearing for the 1982 sales season, this car was christened the Acclaim, with production initially scheduled to be at the Canley works, but later moving to Oxford.

By this time, British Leyland were struggling, being supported year after year by the Government.

In 1983, the organisation became known as the Austin-Rover Group Limited, and in the following year, the Triumph name was used for the last time.

Since then, the name was changed yet again to the Rover Group, a company now owned by British Aerospace. At the time of writing the Canley works continues to be used by the Group for research and development, and a number of smaller concerns rent parts of the factory.

The TR2 production line. Note the Standards in the background.

A TR2 after completing the 1954 Le Mans 24 Hour Race - it finished 15th overall.

The TR3 had a wider grille than the TR2, but was otherwise very similar.

Triumph TR3 on the Liége-Rome-Liége Rally.

The Triumph TR4A, introduced in 1965 and powered by a 2,138cc four-cylinder engine. The six-cylinder TR5 of 1967 had the same bodyshell. This picture is taken from a contemporary sales brochure.

A TRS entered by the works in the Le Mans 24 Hour Race of 1961. It had a special two-litre racing engine nick-named Sabrina, because of its shape bearing more than a passing resemblance to an actress by the same name. It finished 11th overall.

A 1966 example of the Triumph GT6.

The 1961 TR4. Only detail changes were made to the body until January 1969. Note the lack of a waistline moulding, distinguishing the TR4 from later variants.

The Mk.IV Triumph Spitfire.

The TR6 had a totally new body, and was introduced in January 1969. A facelift occured in early 1973.

The extremely attractive Triumph Stag; a three-litre machine built from 1970 to 1977.

TRIUMPH 1800

TR2

TR3

TR3A

TR4

TR4A

The 1300/Toledo proved to be very popular. This is one of the very first Toledo models.

Right: A Dolomite Sprint on the 1977 Mintex Rally. The car produced 125 bhp.

A 1969 2.5 PI - the Triumph 2000 with a TR6 engine.

The 2000/2500 body was modernised in 1973. This is the 2.5 PI model.

The Works Team, ready to depart for the 1970 World Cup Rally.

Above: A works TR7 on the 1979 Manx Rally. 3.5 litre V-8-engined versions were used extensively by the BL Competitions Department, instead of the more usual four-cylinder two-litre models.

The last of the line - the Acclaim. An ironic link with the past came in the early 'eighties when Avon modified the Triumph Acclaim, upgrading the old interior and adding a turbocharger. Few were built, however.

XVI: STANDARD COMMERCIAL VEHICLES

The first production Standard commercial was based on the pre-WWI Light Car chassis, and made its debut in August 1914. Priced at £205, electric lighting was made available for an extra £15.

In 1933, the 20 hp chassis was used by Midland Light Bodies of Coventry as the basis for their ambulance. Most were made for the works, but they were also offered at £435 to outside parties.

Post-WWII, Standard's involvement in com-

1933 20 hp ambulance in Standard works livery.

mercial vehicles became stronger. At the 1948 Motor Show, two new vehicles were announced; the 12cwt delivery van and the 12cwt pick-up truck, both clearly modified Vanguard bodyshells.

For the 1955 season, Standard introduced their 6cwt range, including a van and a pick-up. These were based on the Ten, and proved to be extremely popular.

Gas turbines were developed during the late 1950s, and the idea was later sold on to Auto Diesels Limited. At the same time, a new 2.3 litre diesel engine was launched. It was sold for use in a number of commercial and marine applications, and used extensively in the firm's tractors.

It wasn't until 1958 that the first Atlas machine appeared. Unlike its predecessors in the commercial vehicle field, this Standard was not merely a converted saloon, but a purpose-built one. Powered by a Standard Ten engine, this forward-control van (or pick-up if the customer required it), was a superb design, built for ease of servicing. Unfortunately, the engine was a little too small, limiting the capacity to 10/12cwt, which was naturally rarely adhered to.

In 1960, the problem was solved when the 1.7 litre Ensign engine was fitted, and the Atlas Major was born. The van was priced at £520, whilst the pick-up was available £10 cheaper. For 1961, the 6cwt van based on the Ten (or Pennant), was given an increased capacity, and was now available in either 7cwt or 10cwt guise.

Two totally new van and pick-up models were introduced in September 1962 - the Standard Fifteen and the Twenty. The latter was available with either petrol or diesel power, the diesel unit being the same one that drove the Leyland two-tonner and Scammell Scarab Four mechanical horse. The Twenty had a longer wheelbase and different grille from its smaller counterpart, although by the end of 1965, both were badged as Leylands.

Only Standard Motor Products of Madras - the Indian manufacturers, persisted with the Standard name, continuing to use it well into the 'eighties. They built a whole range of commercial vehicles with load

The 12cwt Vanguard van in Standard Motor Co. livery.

The 12cwt pick-up, again in Standard livery.

The 6cwt van, based on the Standard Ten.

1956 Standard Ten Utilecon.

A 6cwt pick-up from the same period.

The Atlas 10/12cwt van.

1959 Atlas van in Whitbread colours. This was powered by the Standard Ten engine.

Standard Twenty pick-up, 1962. It was later badged as a Leyland.

The Leyland Fifteen van dating from the early 'sixties. The registration is much earlier.

Standard Motor Products of India Limited built this 3.15 tonne vehicle called the Microlorry ...

capacities of up to three tons.

The most successful Standard-built commercial however, has to be the Ferguson tractor. Because of its importance to the postwar development of the Company, we'll look at it in some detail.

The deal struck up with Harry Ferguson just after the Second World War was good for both companies. It gave Ferguson a firm footing in the British market, and Standard some much-needed cash with which they could update production facilities and develop new cars. By September 1946, the first Standard-built Ferguson tractors were leaving Banner Lane - Standard's former Shadow Factory on the outskirts of Coventry. Within five years, over 200,000 Fergusons had been constructed by the Company.

Sociéte Standard-Hotchkiss of St Denis had been formed in 1952 to allow Hotchkiss to assemble Ferguson tractors in France. A licence was later

... they also built this 1983 multi-purpose diesel van.

granted to the Standard-Hotchkiss concern allowing them to build the 23C diesel engine.

In September 1953, Harry Ferguson merged with Massey-Harris to form the famous Massey-

Banner Lane in the early 'fifties - Standard's second Shadow Factory, started in May 1939.

99

Ferguson concern, but production at the Standard works continued unaffected, at least for the time being. 1957 very nearly saw a merger between Massey-Ferguson and Standard, although a so-called "co-ordination committee" had existed since 1955 with three men from each Board. However, at the eleventh hour, the deal was stopped due to a dramatic fall in the former's share value.

In August 1959, the Standard Motor Company and Massey-Ferguson went their separate ways. The tractor firm bought the Banner Lane site, and continued to build their products in large numbers. They also bought Standard-Hotchkiss in France, adding to their empire. In fact, the company is still trading profitably in Banner Lane today.

After Massey-Harris-Ferguson and the Standard Motor Company split up, the Standard Tractor Company was formed, but this concern was liquidated a few months after the British Leyland takeover and before any serious production was underway.

Sir John Black and Harry Ferguson pictured in 1951 with the 200,000th tractor built by Standard, a TE20 model. TE stands for Tractor England, so this was a 20 hp machine built in this country.

Standard-built Ferguson Tractors

Years	Model	Power unit
1946 - 1948	TE20	Continental petrol engine.
1947 - 1956	TEA-20	Standard petrol engine.
1946 - 1948	TEB-20	Continental petrol (narrow track).
1948 - 1956	TEC-20	Standard petrol (narrow track).
1949 - 1956	TED-20	Standard vapourising oil engine.
1949 - 1956	TEE-20	Ditto (narrow track).
1951 - 1956	TEF-20	Diesel engine by Perkins.
1950 - 1956	TEH-20	Standard lamp oil engine.
1950 - 1956	TEJ-20	Ditto (narrow track).
1952 - 1956	TEK-20	Standard petrol (vineyard model).
1952 - 1956	TEL-20	Standard V.O (vineyard model).
1952 - 1956	TEM-20	Standard lamp oil (vineyard model).
1952 - 1956	TEP-20	Standard petrol (industrial model).
1952 - 1956	TER-20	Standard V.O (industrial model).
1952 - 1956	TES-20	Standard lamp oil (industrial).
1952 - 1956	TET-20	Standard diesel (industrial).
1956 - 1958	FE35	Standard petrol, V.O or diesel.
1958 - 1959	MF35	Standard petrol, V.O or diesel.

XVII: MADE FROM STANDARD PARTS

The number of companies who have based their cars on Standard components may surprise the reader, it certainly surprised the author!

By far the most famous concern to use Standard parts has to be SS Cars Limited. This company developed from the Swallow Coachbuilding Company of Blackpool, who made motorcycle sidecars and new bodies for popular small cars of the nineteen-twenties.

The man behind Swallow was William Lyons, later Sir William. He moved his business to Coventry in 1928, and shortly afterwards made his first contact with the Standard Motor Company. The Standard-Swallow of 1929 was the result. Based on the 9 hp chassis, it was the first of many such projects which ran into 1932 - the year in which the first production SS made its debut; SS being a name used for the new cars built by Swallow.

SS Cars Limited was formed in October 1933, although the company continued to buy its engines and chassis from Standard. This arrangement continued until the outbreak of the Second World War, although the SS-Jaguar models gradually moved away from Canley-built chassis, and the engines were often tuned by Weslake.

After the War, Jaguar Cars Limited was born, but only the 1.8 litre engine continued to be bought in from Standard. Sir John Black had sold the tooling for the larger engines to Jaguar, and when he offered to buy it back, Lyons is said to have answered: "Thanks, John, but I've got the ball now, and I'll kick it myself if you don't mind." Within three years, Jaguar was totally independent, building everything in-house, and the rest, as they say, is history ...

Avon could be included in this chapter, but it is fairer to say that they were specialist coachbuilders,

as their cars never really tried to lose their Standard identity, unlike the machines built by William Lyons, which were actively marketed as something different. The same is true, of course, of the Patrick-bodied vehicles.

The Jensen brothers, however, although linked with both Avon and Patrick Motors, did build their own cars as well. The first Jensen was based on the Austin Seven, but it caught the eye of Alfred Wilde, who immediately asked the pair to design a similar car for Standard. The idea was taken up, and Avon carried out the coachbuilding. Further cars, not linked with Standard, were built following the great success of the model, and despite a chequered history, Jensen was still trading at the time of writing.

Raymond Mays, the man behind such enterprises as ERA and BRM, was an avid supporter of the Standard marque. He was one of the few people who could see the potential of the pre-war Standard V-8 engine, and built a short series of cars based on the V-8 chassis. These were both fast and elegant machines but, sadly, few were built. It should be noted that Mays got the Standard Motor Company involved in the V-16 BRM project as well, with a number of components being built at Canley.

Railton was a make founded in 1933 by Noel Campbell Macklin, after his ambitions with Invicta

AVON COUPE—SIX CYLINDER SIXTEEN CHASSIS

Avon models, like this coupé, were highly regarded by sports car enthusiasts.

faded away. The designer of the new car was Reid Railton, hence the name. Although the majority of Railton cars were large-engined machines, in 1938, Railton introduced the "Baby Railton", based on Standard Ten running gear. About fifty of these models were built.

Morgan, another sports car manufacturer, also bought its four-cylinder engines from Standard just before and after the War. Before it, Morgan used the 1,267cc unit to power its 4/4 model, and after it, the 2.1 litre Vanguard engine propelled the Plus 4.

The Jensen brothers got their break into the industry by designing a car for the Standard Motor Company - here it is, the 1929 Avon Special.

One of the Raymond Mays Specials. Five cars were built from 1938 to 1939, but then the War intervened. Three of them ran in the 1939 RAC Rally, driven by Mays himself, Sammy Davis, and C. M. Anthony.

The second series SSI sports saloon, powered by Standard.

The Baby Railton which used many Standard Ten components.

It is interesting to note that, in 1954, Standard offered to buy the Morgan concern but its offer was rejected. However, engines were still supplied up until 1968, these being TR units.

Early postwar Lea-Francis cars used the Standard-built gearboxes, before turning to Moss units, and the V-8 chassis had been supplied to AC Cars in the late 'thirties.

Peerless and Warwick, although originally totally different marques, were, in later years, one and the same. Peerless was an American company founded way back in 1900, but due to the luxury cars it built, was killed off by the Great Depression.

A concern selling Peerless spares in England was formed just after the First World War, becoming the agency for Jaguar and Hudson cars as the years passed. In 1957, the garage was bought by Mr J. Byrnes who financed the production of a new car, the Peerless GT. This model was powered by the TR3 engine, and was built between 1958 and 1960, with around 350 leaving the works. Up to fifty more were built in the following two years, although these later cars carried the Warwick badge.

Fairthorpe built small glassfibre-bodied specials from 1954 to 1978. Triumph engines were used by the company extensively, ranging from the 1.3 litre, through to the 1.6, 2.0, and 2.5 litre units. The latter engines were perhaps a little too powerful for such a light car.

Imperia of Liége, after finishing building their own cars in 1949, moved into building Vanguards under licence. They not only built unmodified versions, but an attractive convertible model as well, one of which has been recently brought to Britain.

The Suisse was the Swiss-built version of the Vanguard and, naturally, there were others dotted around the globe. In India, links with Standard continued even after the Company's death. From 1961 to 1980, Standard Motor Products of Madras built the Herald, and named it the Gazel.

Bond, founded in 1948, built a model called the Equipé in 1963. This had a Herald chassis, a Spitfire engine and a glassfibre body. It was built with the full co-operation of the Company, and was joined in 1968-69 by a 2.0-litre version, before the firm was taken over by Reliant.

The Dove GTR4 (1963 - 1964), was a tasteful fastback conversion of the TR4 by Dove's of Wim-

Below: Buttercup - a highly successful trials car based on the pre-war Standard. During the 'fifties, it won several important events, and, according to Harry Webster, inspired the Company to produce the TR1 prototype that led to the TR2.

The car shown in the inset is a recently-completed vehicle built in the same spirit.

Morgan made good use of Standard power units after the Second World War.

Power graced by elegance

SPEED Packed into the 2 litre engine of the Swallow Doretti is all the surging power needed to send the miles scudding behind. Although capable of over 100 miles an hour the car is ideal for fast touring at 75 to 90 m.p.h., at the same time high performance is combined with exceptionally economical running.

COMFORT Controls and steering are so arranged to give maximum comfort for the driver, while the interior is luxuriously fitted with leather covered sponge rubber moulding, first quality hide upholstery and thick carpeting.

SAFETY The 50-ton tubular steel chassis of the Swallow Doretti is specially built to meet the stresses of high-speed motoring and to ensure the greatest possible stability; hydraulic brakes are also fitted, thus you can drive this fine car knowing that every device to provide the greatest possible safety has been incorporated.

STYLE Friends will stop and admire the smooth, sleek lines of your Swallow Doretti. Beautifully styled on the classical Sports Car lines it provides the utmost in elegance.

Swallow Doretti

The sports car you will be proud to own

Price £777.0s.0d. P.T. £324.17s.6d.
For name of nearest Distributor write or phone to:
THE SWALLOW COACHBUILDING COMPANY (1935) LTD.
The Airport, Walsall, Staffs. Walsall 4553

ABOVE is shown the luxurious interior of the Swallow Doretti with controls neatly grouped in front of the driver, while LEFT shows the 50-ton tubular steel chassis that ensures complete stability.

Period advertising for the Swallow Doretti, August 1954.

bledon - an official Triumph distributor.

Even Saab bought in Triumph engines for their Model 99 machines, launched towards the end of 1969. Over the years that followed, it was progressively enlarged from 1.7 to 1.8 litres, and finally two-litres. It is interesting to note that the head of the Saab car division was Gunnar Ljungstrom, an ex-Standard man, and that the slant-four found favour over a similar Ricardo unit.

TVR and Marcos also used Triumph engines during the early 'seventies, as did Panther and Trident. The Lubeck-built Amphicar was another Triumph engine user.

However, it was the Swallow Doretti project that was the most interesting of all from a Standard-Triumph point of view, not only because it used the firm's components, but because it very nearly became a part of the Company's range.

Designed by Frank Rainbow, it was aimed at the sports car enthusiast who wanted a little more comfort than the TR2 could offer. Black saw the opportunity for sales in the 'States, from where the idea originated, and wanted to take the Doretti onboard. However, he had an accident whilst testing the car with Ken Richardson, and that brought the idea to an end - as well as Black's career.

Naturally, one cannot forget the post-1963 Triumphs as, after all is said and done, the majority of these were Standards under the skin.

We know it's astronauts' language
but . . .

for **EYEBALLS-IN** *ACCELERATION,*

for **EYEBALLS-OUT** *BRAKING,*

for **HIGH "G" CORNERING**

YOU MUST DRIVE A

FAIRTHORPE-TECHNICAL EXPONENTS

TX-GT

PRICE Basic **£1064,** UK **£1309** ; kits from **£954**
FOR A TEST DRIVE CONTACT FAIRTHORPE LTD.
Denham Green Lane, Denham, Bucks.   Denham 2409

Fairthorpe had links with Standard and Triumph from their earliest days. The TX-GT used any of the larger Triumph engines, and was introduced in 1968.

The styling of the Warwick and Peerless cars would have been much improved minus the fins on the wings and roof.

The Bond Equipe, this example dating from 1967.

The Standard Gazel, produced in India well into the 'eighties, and clearly based on the Herald. Note the four doors, the simplified bonnet, and Vitesse-style grille.

All-British Standard MOTOR COMPANY LIMITED CANLEY ——— COVENTRY

XVIII: THE SPECIALIST COACHBUILDERS

Many legends were born in pre-war days, and much of a company's reputation is down to its coachbuilders. One only has to think of Alfa Romeo and Ferrari and, instantly, visions of Pininfarina and Touring bodies are pictured. Alternatively, think of Delahaye and Delage, and Chapron and Figoni & Falaschi come to mind. Although perhaps not quite as glamorous as these, Standard did have their moments, especially in the years between the wars.

Although many Standard bodies, in fact the vast majority, were built either in-house or by tied concerns such as Fisher & Ludlow, specialist coachbuilders were called on for a number of models.

More often than not with Standard, coachbuilt vehicles were listed as stock items, as they would commission new designs and call them off as they were needed. Typical examples of this include the 1933 Twenty Landaulette by Mulliner, the 1935 Dorchester saloon by Samuel Holbrook of Wolverhampton or, naturally, the Avon creations. It was only really the very early cars that carried one-off bodies by the likes of Windovers or Vincents, so we shall look at the more popular firms who worked with Standard.

By far the most important coachbuilder associated with the Standard Motor Company was Avon of Warwick. Founded in the early 'twenties, Avon was responsible for bringing glamour to the marque in the 'thirties.

The company's somewhat chequered history came to an end only very recently, the works concentrating on Volvo cars.

In its earlier days, the Patrick Motor Group was better known for tts coachbuilding skills rather than their string of petrol stations and dealerships throughout the Midlands.

Founded in 1930 as Edgbaston Garages Limited, by the mid-thirties, the company was an established coachbuilder, having links with Standard, Austin, Wolseley, and the Jensen brothers. Sadly, Patrick-bodied cars are now very rare.

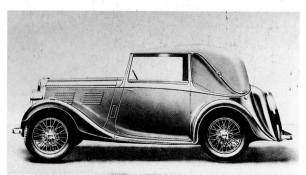

Tickford, or Salmons-Tickford, date back to 1820. It was always the Tickford folding head that the company was famous for, finding its way onto many superb chassis such as Alvis, Humber and Lagonda, as well as Standard, of course. In 1957, the business was taken-over by Aston Martin.

The Swallow Coachbuilding Company of Blackpool, and later Coventry, was founded by William Lyons. He built his business up by putting sporting bodies on the popular chassis of the day. The decision to use the Standard frame was one of his most important, as it formed the basis for the SS marque, which in time became Jaguar, of course.

No relation to H. J. Mulliner of London, or Mulliner of Northampton, for that matter, the Mulliner that the Standard Company used was the Birmingham-based concern.
Founded in the 18th century, it was taken-over by Standard in 1958, together with its subsidiary the Forward Radiator Co.

Imperia was a Belgian company which built Standards under licence during the 'fifties. Its first car had been built in 1906, although from 1950, only Vanguards were produced. However, the company deserves inclusion in this section of the book, as it was the only one to build the superb Vanguard Convertible.

IMPERIA S. A. NESSONVAUX PRÉSENTE
Le Cabriolet Vanguard " Nessonvaux " 1955

Giovanni Michelotti and his team did a lot of work for the Standard-Triumph organisation, including the design of the famous Herald. Vignale did most of his coachwork, as he worked for this company for a number of years.

Standard
MOTOR COMPANY LIMITED
CANLEY ——————— COVENTRY

XIX: PRODUCTION MODELS - DATES & DATA

This chapter lists every Standard and Triumph motor car ever built. The Standard cars are listed first, then the Triumphs. Purely for interest, pre-war Triumphs are included.

Reading from left to right, the columns carry the following information: Years, Model, Number of Cylinders, Bore & Stroke, Cubic Capacity, Valve Arrangement, Wheelbase, Track, Length and Width.

			Pre-WWI Standards						
1903	6 hp	1	5" x 3"	1006	Side	6'6"			
1904-1905	12/15	2	5" x 3"	1926	Side				
1904	3-cylinder	3							
1905	16 hp	4	100 x 100	3142	Side	9'0"			
1905-1908	18/20	6	100 x 100	4714	Side	10'0"			
1906	10 hp	2	70 x 82	631	Side	6'6"	4'0"	9'3"	
1906	16/20	4	102 x 108	3531	Side	9'0"	4'6"	13'6"	5'0"
1906	16/20	4	102 x 108	3531	Side	10'0"	4'6"	13'6"	5'0"
1906	24/30	6	4" x 4"	5232	Side	10'0"	4'6"	14'6"	5'0"
1906	24/30	6	4" x 4"	5232	Side	11'0"	4'6"	14'6"	5'0"
1906 -1912	50 hp	6	140 x 127	11734	Side	11'0"	4'8"	15'0"	5'6"
1906 -1912	50 hp	6	140 x 127	11734	Side	12'0"	4'8"	15'0"	5'6"
1906	Air-cooled "Lindsay"	4							
1906	Air-cooled "Bradburn"	6							
1907	15 hp	6	70 x 82	1593	Side	7'3"	4'0"	10'0"	4'6"
1907	30 hp Model B	6	102 x 108	5297	Side	10'0"	4'6"	14'6"	5'0"
1908	30 hp Model D	6	102 x 108	5297	Side	10'0"	4'6"	14'6"	5'0"
1908-1911	20 hp	6	89 x 108	4032	Side	9'8"	4'8"	13'0"	5'3"
1908-1911	40 hp	6	102 x 127	6167	Side	10'0"	4'8"	14'2"	5'6"
1908-1911	40 hp	6	102 x 127	6167	Side	11'0"	4'8"	14'2"	5'6"
1909	14 hp								
1909-1911	16 hp	4	89 x 108	2688	Side	9'2"	4'8"	12'0"	5'3"
1909-1911	16 hp	4	89 x 108	2688	Side	10'0"	4'8"	12'0"	5'3"
1910-1911	12 hp Model J	4	68 x 114	1656	Side	8'0"	4'8"	11'3"	5'3"
1911	15 hp	6	79 x 114						
1911-1912	20 hp	6	80 x 120	3620	Side	10'6"	4'8"	14'4"	5'4"
1912	15 hp Model K	4	80 x 120	2368	Side	10'0"	4'9"	13'6"	5'6"
1912	25 hp	6	89 x 108	4032	Side	10'6"	4'8"	14'6"	5'4"
1913-1914	20 hp	4	89 x 133	3336	Side	10'1"	4'9"	13'1"	5'6"
1913-1914	20 hp	4	89 x 133	3336	Side	10'7"	4'9"	14'6"	5'6"
1913-1915	9.5 hp Model S	4	62 x 90	1087	Side	7'6"	4'0"	10'6"	

			Vintage Standards						
1918	9.5 hp Model S	4	62 x 90	1087	Side	7'6"	4'0"	10'6"	
1919-1921	9.5 hp SLS	4	62 x 110	1328	Side	7'8"	4'0"	10'9"	
1921-1923	8 hp	4	62 x 90	1087	Ohv	8'6"	4'0"	11'4"	4'10"
1921-1923	11.6 hp SLO	4	68 x 110	1598	Ohv	9'0"	4'6"	12'7"	5'8"
1922-1926	13.9 hp SLO-4	4	75 x 110	1944	Ohv	9'8"	4'3"	13'9"	5'7"
1923-1927	11.4 hp V3	4	68 x 90	1307	Ohv	8'9"	4'3"	12'0"	5'3"
1926-1928	13.9 hp V4	4	75 x 110	1944	Ohv	9'8"	4'3"	13'9"	5'7"

Years	Model	Cyl	Bore x Stroke	Cap	Valve				
1927	12/24			1944					
1927-1928	14/28			1944					
1927-1928	18/36 hp 6-V	6	68 x 102	2230	Ohv	10'2"	4'8"	14'3"	5'10"
1928	18/24 hp 6-V	6	68 x 102	2230	Ohv	10'2"	4'8"	14'3"	5'10"
1927-1929	9 hp	4	60 x 102	1153	Side	7'7"	3'9"	11'4"	4'9"
1928-1930	9 hp Lwb	4	63 x 102	1287	Side	8'3"	3'9"	12'7"	4'9"
1929-1931	15 hp Swb	6	63 x 102	1930	Side	9'3"	4'6"	14'1"	5'6"
1929-1930	15 hp "Envoy"	6	65 x 102	2054	Side	9'10"	4'8"	14'8"	5'8"

Post-Vintage Standards

Years	Model	Cyl	Bore x Stroke	Cap	Valve				
1929-1931	15 hp Swb	6	63 x 102	1930	Side	9'3"	4'6"	14'1"	5'6"
1930-1933	15 hp Lwb	6	65 x 102	2054	Side	9'10"	4'8"	14'8"	5'8"
1930-1933	9.9 hp Big Nine	4	63 x 102	1287	Side	8'3"	3'8"	12'2"	5'0"
1931-1935	20 hp "Envoy"	6	73 x 102	2552	Side	9'10"	4'8"	15'8"	5'10"
1932-1933	Little Nine	4	60 x 88	1006	Side	7'7"	3'8"	11'0"	4'5"
1932-1933	Little Twelve	6	57 x 87	1337	Side	8'1"	3'8"	11'7"	4'5"
1932-1933	Big Twelve	6	60 x 87	1497	Side	8'5"	4'2"	12'2"	5'0"
1934	12/6 Twelve-Six	6	60 x 87	1497	Side	8'6"	4'4"	13'2"	5'1"
1934-1935	10/12 Speed Model	4	69 x 106	1608	Side	8'6"	3'10"	12'6"	4'7"
1934-1936	Nine	4	60 x 92	1052	Side	7'3"	3'8"	11'5"	4'7"
1934-1936	Nine	4	60 x 92	1052	Side	7'6"	3'8"	11'5"	4'7"
1934-1936	Ten	4	63 x 106	1343	Side	7'7"	3'10"	12'0"	4'7"
1934-1936	Ten	4	63 x 106	1343	Side	7'10"	3'10"	12'0"	4'7"
1934	Twelve	4	69 x 106	1608	Side	8'6"	4'4"	13'2"	5'1"
1934-1936	Sixteen	6	63 x 106	2143	Side	8'11"	4'8"	14'0"	5'5"
1935	Twelve	4	69 x 106	1608	Side	8'6"	4'4"	13'5"	5'1"
1935-1936	Twenty	6	73 x 106	2664	Side	9'9"	4'9"	14'6"	5'10"
1935-1936	Twenty	6	73 x 106	2664	Side	10'3"	4'9"	14'6"	5'10"
1936	Twelve	4	69 x 106	1608	Side	8'3"	4'4"	13'4"	5'1"
1936	Light Twelve	4	69 x 106	1608	Side	8'6"	3'10"	12'6"	4'7"
1936	Light Twenty	6	73 x 106	2664	Side	8'11"	4'8"	14'0"	5'5"

Flying Standards

Years	Model	Cyl	Bore x Stroke	Cap	Valve				
1935-1936	Flying Twelve	4	69 x 106	1608	Side	9'0"			
1935-1936	Flying Sixteen	6	63 x 106	2143	Side	9'8"			
1935-1939	Flying Twenty	6	73 x 106	2664	Side	9'8"	4'4"	15'0"	5'3"
1936	Flying Ten	4	63 x 106	1343	Side	8'4"	4'0"	13'7"	4'11"
1936	Flying Light Twelve	4	69 x 106	1608	Side	8'4"	4'0"	13'7"	4'11"
1936-1937	20 hp V-8	8	63 x 106	2686	Side	8'6"	4'4"	13'9"	5'3"
1937-1938	20 hp V-8	8	63 x 106	2686	Side	8'6"	4'4"	14'2"	5'3"
1937-1938	Flying Ten	4	63 x 100	1267	Side	7'6"	4'0"	12'6"	4'11"
1937-1939	Flying Twelve	4	69 x 106	1608	Side	8'4"	4'0"	13'7"	4'11"
1937-1940	Flying Nine	4	60 x 100	1131	Side	7'1"	3'10"	12'3"	4'8"
1937-1940	Flying Light Twelve	4	63 x 106	1343	Side	8'4"	4'0"	13'7"	4'11"
1937-1940	Flying Fourteen	4	69 x 106	1608	Side	9'0"	4'4"	14'5"	5'2"
1937-1940	Flying Fourteen	4	73 x 106	1776	Side	9'0"	4'4"	14'5"	5'2"
1937-1940	Flying Twenty	6	63 x 106	2143	Side	9'8"	4'4"	15'0"	5'3"
1938-1940	Flying Eight (2dr)	4	57 x 100	1021	Side	6'11"	3'9"	11'7"	4'7"
1939	Flying Ten	4	63 x 100	1267	Side	7'6"	3'10"	12'8"	4'8"
1939	Flying Twelve De Luxe	4	69 x 106	1608	Side	8'4"	4'3"	13'9"	4'11"
1939-1940	Flying Eight (4dr)	4	57 x 100	1021	Side	7'4"	3'9"	12'0"	4'7"
1939-1940	Flying Ten Super	4	63 x 100	1267	Side	7'6"	4'0"	12'6"	4'10"
1939-1940	Flying Twelve	4	69 x 106	1608	Side	8'4"	4'3"	13'9"	5'0"
1939-1940	Flying Twelve DHC	4	69 x 106	1608	Side	8'4"	4'2"	13'9"	5'0"

1945-1948	Eight (4-8A)	4	57 x 100	1021	Side	6'11"	3'9"	11'7"	4'8"
1945-1948	Twelve (12CD)	4	69 x 106	1608	Side	8'4"	4'6"	13'9"	5'3"
1945-1948	Fourteen (14CD)	4	73 x 106	1776	Side	8'4"	4'6"	13'9"	5'3"

Vanguard and Vanguard-based Models

1947	Vanguard Phase I	4	80 x 92	1849	Ohv	7'10"	4'6"	13'10"	5'9"
1948-1951	Vanguard Phase I	4	85 x 92	2088	Ohv	7'10"	4'6"	13'10"	5'9"
1951-1953	Vanguard Phase IA	4	85 x 92	2088	Ohv	7'10"	4'6"	13'10"	5'9"
1953-1955	Vanguard Phase II	4	85 x 92	2088	Ohv	7'10"	4'6"	13'10"	5'9"
1954-1955	Vanguard Ph.II Diesel	4	81 x 102	2092	Ohv	7'10"	4'6"	13'10"	5'9"
1955-1958	Vanguard Phase III	4	85 x 92	2088	Ohv	8'6"	4'3"	14'3"	5'7"
1956-1957	Sportsman	4	85 x 92	2088	Ohv	8'6"	4'3"	14'5"	5'7"
1957-1961	Ensign	4	76 x 92	1670	Ohv	8'6"	4'3"	14'3"	5'7"
1957-1961	Ensign Diesel	4	81 x 102	2092	Ohv	8'6"	4'3"	14'3"	5'7"
1958-1961	Phase III Vignale	4	85 x 92	2088	Ohv	8'6"	4'3"	14'3"	5'7"
1961-1963	Phase III Six	6	75 x 76	1998	Ohv	8'6"	4'3"	14'5"	5'7"
1962-1963	Ensign II De Luxe	4	86 x 92	2138	Ohv	8'6"	4'3"	14'3"	5'7"

Eights and Tens

1953-1955	Eight	4	58 x 76	803	Ohv	7'0"	4'0"	12'0"	5'0"
1954-1955	Eight De Luxe	4	58 x 76	803	Ohv	7'0"	4'0"	12'0"	5'0"
1954-1955	Ten	4	63 x 76	948	Ohv	7'0"	4'0"	12'0"	5'0"
1955-1962	Companion	4	63 x 76	948	Ohv	7'0"	4'0"	12'0"	5'0"
1955-1956	Eight Family Saloon	4	58 x 76	803	Ohv	7'0"	4'0"	12'0"	5'0"
1955-1957	Eight Super Saloon	4	58 x 76	803	Ohv	7'0"	4'0"	12'0"	5'0"
1955-1956	Ten Super Saloon	4	63 x 76	948	Ohv	7'0"	4'0"	12'0"	5'0"
1956-1957	Eight Family Ph.II	4	58 x 76	803	Ohv	7'0"	4'0"	12'0"	5'0"
1956-1957	Ten Family Saloon	4	63 x 76	948	Ohv	7'0"	4'0"	12'0"	5'0"
1956-1957	Ten Super Ph.II	4	63 x 76	948	Ohv	7'0"	4'0"	12'0"	5'0"
1957-1959	Eight Gold Star	4	58 x 76	803	Ohv	7'0"	4'0"	12'0"	5'0"
1957-1959	Ten Gold Star	4	63 x 76	948	Ohv	7'0"	4'0"	12'0"	5'0"
1957-1959	Pennant	4	63 x 76	948	Ohv	7'0"	4'0"	11'10"	4'11"

Standard Commercials and Wartime Vehicles

1940-1941	Beaverette I/II	4	73 x 106	1776	Side				
1940-1944	12 hp Light Utility	4	69 x 106	1608	Side	9'0"	4'1"	13'7"	5'2"
1941-1943	Beaverette III/IV	4	73 x 106	1776	Side	6'2"	4'3"	10'2"	5'10"
1943	Jeep	4	69 x 106	1608	Side				
1944	Jungle Bug	4	57 x 100	1021	Side				
1945	4wd Agricultural	4		1009					
1946	Ferguson Tractors only								
1947-1958	12cwt	4	85 x 92	2088	Ohv				
1954-1962	6cwt	4	63 x 76	948	Ohv				
1958-1962	10 hp Atlas	4	63 x 76	948	Ohv	7'0"	3'9"	13'4"	5'7"
1962-1963	Atlas Major	4	76 x 92	1670	Ohv	7'0"	3'9"	12'7"	4'7"
1962-1965	7cwt	4	69 x 76	1147	Ohv				

Note: Ferguson Tractors listed in chapter 15.

Pre-War Triumphs

1923-1926	10/20	1934	Gloria Six
1923-1926	10/20 Sports	1935-1937	Gloria 10.8 Four
1924-1926	13/35	1935-1936	Gloria-Vitesse
1926-1930	15	1935-1936	Gloria Six Mk.II
1927-1932	Super Seven	1935-1936	Gloria-Vitesse Six
1931-1932	Scorpion	1937	Gloria 1.5 litre
1932-1933	Twelve/Six	1937	Continental Two-Litre
1932-1933	Super Nine	1937-1939	Dolomite Two-Litre
1932	Southern Cross 8.9 hp	1937-1939	Dolomite 14/60
1933-1934	Southern Cross 9.9 hp	1937-1938	Vitesse Two-Litre
1933-1934	Super Eight	1937-1938	Vitesse 14/60
1933-1934	Ten	1938	Gloria Fourteen
1934-1936	Gloria 9.5 Four	1938-1939	Dolomite 1.5 litre
1934-1935	Gloria Monte Carlo	1939	Twelve
1934-1935	Dolomite Straight-Eight	1939	Dolomite 14/65

Standard-built Triumphs

1946-1948	1800 Roadster	4	73 x 106	1776	Ohv	8'4"	4'2"	14'0"	5'4"
1946-1949	1800 Saloon	4	73 x 106	1776	Ohv	9'0"	4'2"	14'7"	5'3"
1948-1949	Roadster	4	85 x 92	2088		8'4"	4'2"	14'0"	5'4"
1949	2000 Saloon	4	85 x 92	2088		9'0"	4'2"	14'7"	5'3"
1949-1952	Renown Mk.I	4	85 x 92	2088		9'0"	4'2"	14'7"	5'3"
1949-1953	Mayflower Saloon	4	63 x 100	1247	Side	7'0"	3'9"	12'10"	5'2"
1949-1953	Mayflower Dhc	4	63 x 100	1247	Side	7'0"	3'9"	12'10"	5'2"
1950	TRX	4	85 x 92	2088	Ohv	7'10"	4'2"	13'10"	5'10"
1951-1952	Renown Limousine	4	85 x 92	2088		9'3"	4'2"	15'1"	5'3"
1952	"TR1"	4	83 x 92	1991	Ohv	7'4"	3'9"	11'9"	4'7"
1952-1954	Renown Mk.II	4	85 x 92	2088		9'3"	4'2"	15'1"	5'3"
1953-1955	TR2	4	83 x 92	1991	Ohv	7'4"	3'9"	12'7"	4'7"
1955-1957	TR3	4	83 x 92	1991	Ohv	7'4"	3'9"	12'7"	4'7"
1957-1960	10 hp Pennant	4	83 x 92	948	Ohv	7'0"	4'0"	11'10"	5'0"
1957-1960	10 hp Ten Sedan	4	63 x 76	948	Ohv	7'0"	4'0"	12'0"	5'0"
1957-1961	TR3A	4	83 x 92	1991	Ohv	7'4"	3'9"	12'7"	4'7"
1958-1959	10 hp Estate Wagon	4	63 x 76	948	Ohv	7'0"	4'0"	12'0"	5'0"
1959-1961	Herald Saloon	4	63 x 76	948	Ohv	7'7"	4'0"	12'9"	5'0"
1959-1961	Herald Coupé	4	63 x 76	948	Ohv	7'7"	4'0"	12'9"	5'0"
1959-1963	Italia	4	83 x 92	1991	Ohv				

Note: Any Triumph cars the production of which started after 1960 have been listed separately on the following page as Leyland-built machines.

Leyland-built Triumphs

1957-1961	TR3A	4	83 x 92	1991	Ohv	7'4"	3'9"	12'7"	4'7"
1959-1961	Herald Saloon	4	63 x 76	948	Ohv	7'7"	4'0"	12'9"	5'0"
1959-1961	Herald Coupé	4	63 x 76	948	Ohv	7'7"	4'0"	12'9"	5'0"
1959-1963	Italia	4	83 x 92	1991	Ohv				
1960-1961	Herald Convertible	4	63 x 76	948	Ohv	7'7"	4'0"	12'9"	5'0"
1961-1962	TR3B	4	86 x 92	2138	Ohv	7'4"	3'9"	12'7"	4'7"
1961-1965	TR4	4	86 x 92	2138	Ohv	7'4"	4'1"	12'9"	4'9"
1961-1968	Herald 1200 Saloon	4	69 x 76	1147	Ohv	7'7"	4'0"	12'9"	5'0"
1961-1968	Herald 1200 Coupé	4	69 x 76	1147	Ohv	7'7"	4'0"	12'9"	5'0"
1961-1968	Herald 1200 Conv.	4	69 x 76	1147	Ohv	7'7"	4'0"	12'9"	5'0"
1961-1968	Herald 1200 Estate	4	69 x 76	1147	Ohv	7'7"	4'0"	12'9"	5'0"
1962-1965	Spitfire Mk.I	4	69 x 76	1147	Ohv	6'11"	4'1"	12'1"	4'9"
1962-1966	Vitesse Saloon	6	67 x 76	1596	Ohv	7'5"	4'1"	12'9"	5'0"
1962-1966	Vitesse Convertible	6	67 x 76	1596	Ohv	7'5"	4'1"	12'9"	5'0"
1962-1967	Herald 12/50	4	69 x 76	1147	Ohv	7'7"	4'0"	12'9"	5'0"
1963-1969	2000 Mk.I Saloon	6	75 x 76	1998	Ohv	8'10"	4'2"	14'5"	5'5"
1963-1969	2000 Mk.I Estate	6	75 x 76	1998	Ohv	8'10"	4'2"	14'5"	5'5"

Post-1963 Triumphs

1965-1967	Spitfire Mk.II
1965-1967	TR4A
1965-1970	1300 Saloon
1966-1968	GT6 Mk.I
1966-1968	Vitesse two-litre Saloon
1966-1968	Vitesse two-litre Convertible
1967-1968	TR5
1967-1968	TR250
1967-1970	Spitfire Mk.III
1967-1970	1300 TC Saloon
1967-1971	Herald 13/60 Saloon
1967-1971	Herald 13/60 Convertible
1967-1971	Herald 13/60 Estate
1968-1969	2.5 PI Mk.I
1968-1970	GT6 Mk.II
1968-1971	Vitesse two-litre Mk.II Saloon
1968-1971	Vitesse two-litre Mk.II Convertible
1969-1975	2.5 PI Mk.II Saloon
1969-1975	2.5 PI Mk.II Estate
1969-1975	TR6
1969-1977	2000 Mk.II Saloon
1969-1977	2000 Mk.II Estate
1970-1977	Stag Convertible
1970-1977	Stag Coupé
1970-1973	GT6 Mk.III
1970-1974	Spitfire Mk.IV
1970-1973	1500 Saloon
1970-1976	Toledo
1972-1976	Dolomite
1973-1976	1500 TC Saloon
1973-1980	Dolomite Sprint
1974-1977	2500 TC Saloon
1974-1977	2500 TC Estate
1975-1977	2500 S Saloon
1975-1977	2500 S Estate
1975-1980	Spitfire 1500
1975-1981	TR7
1976-1980	Dolomite 1300
1976-1980	Dolomite 1500
1976-1980	1850 HL
1980-1981	TR8
1981-1984	Acclaim

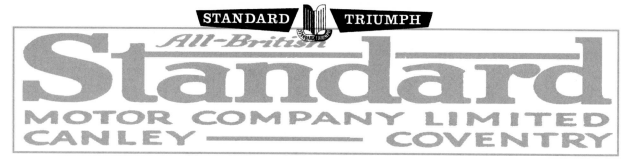

XX: CLUBS, LITERATURE & COLLECTIONS

Clubs

The Standard Motor Club, founded in 1973, is the only club that caters for the whole range of Standard cars and, of course, their many derivatives. Its aims are to promote interest in, use of and preservation of all Standard and Standard-based vehicles. The Club provides a forty page magazine ten times a year, as well as free technical advice, help with spares, a library facility, and numerous social events throughout the year.

Membership details can be obtained from; *Tony Pingriff, 57 Main Road, Meriden, nr Coventry, CV7 7LP.*

There are only two other Standard clubs based in England, the Phase I and II Vanguard Owners Club, and the Standard-Triumph Register. The first of these offers a quarterly newsletter, remanufactured spares, and technical back-up for the owner, as well as an annual National Rally, whilst the well-established Register holds rallies and collates information on the older surviving machines.

Vanguard Club details can be obtained from; *Mr P. J. Barclay, c/o The Villa, 11 The Down, Alveston, BS12 2PH.*

Triumph Clubs are far more numerous, and include the Triumph Sports Six Club. This is the largest of the Owners Clubs, covering the Herald, Spitfire, GT6, Vitesse, and any other Herald-based vehicle.

Membership details can be obtained from; *121b St Mary's Road, Market Harborough, Leics.*

The TR Register is the next largest organisation and, as the name suggests, deals with the whole Triumph TR range.

Membership details can be obtained from; *Mrs R. Good, 271 High Street, Berkhamstead, HP4 1AA.*

There is also the TR Drivers Club.

Membership details can be obtained from; *Mrs Donna Cross, 108 Bursledon Road, Southampton, SO2 7LZ.*

The Triumph Sporting Owners Club welcomes any Triumph motor car and, like many of the Triumph Clubs, has a motorsport calendar in addition to the usual facilities.

Membership details can be obtained from; *Richard King, 16 Windsor Road, Hazel Grove, Stockport, SK7 4SW.*

The popularity of the Triumph Stag never ceases to amaze. An Owners Club purely for this model was formed in 1979, and continues to be very active

Membership details can be obtained from; *John Ramsden, Cedar Cottage, Melpash, Bridport,*

Members of the Standard Motor Club at an event organised at the Canley works. Sadly, the future of this great landmark is now in question.

DT6 3UH.

Other one model Clubs include the Triumph Roadster Club for 1946 to 1949 models.

Membership details can be obtained from;
Mr H Gillott, The Woodlands, Taddington, nr Buxton, SK17 9UD.

The Triumph Mayflower Club for all Mayflowers built between 1949 and 1954.

Membership details can be obtained from;
Mr T. Gordon, 12 Manor Close, Hoghton, Preston, PR5 0EN.

The Triumph Razoredge Owners Club for the 1800, 2000, and Renown saloons and limousines built between 1946 and 1954.

Membership details can be obtained from;
Chris Hewitt, Woodhall, The Highlands, Leatherhead, KT24 5BQ.

The Triumph 1300 Register for the fwd models produced between 1966 and 1973, both 1.3 and 1.5 litre machines.

Membership details can be obtained from;
Steve Waldenberg, 39 Winding Way, Leeds, LS17 7RG.

The Dolomite Sprint Register - obviously for the Sprint, but also catering for the basic Dolomite, 1300, 1500 and so on.

Membership details can be obtained from;
Paul Edgington, 39 Mill Lane, Arncott, Bicester, OX6 0PB.

The Triumph 2000/2500/2.5 Register, which covers all the big saloons and estates from 1963 to 1977.

Membership details can be obtained from;
Mr G. Aldous, 42 Hall Orchards, Middleton, Kings Lynn, PE32 1RY.

There is also the Pre-1940 Triumph Owners Club. Club membership is currently at around 250.

Membership details can be obtained from;
Roy Potton, 15 Hawthorn Way, Chiswell Green, St Albans, AL2 3BG.

Catering for all Triumph models by area are the Club Triumph North London.

Membership details can be obtained from;
Derek Pollock, 86 Waggon Road, Hadley Wood, Herts., EN4 0PP.

And also Club Triumph Eastern.

Membership details can be obtained from;
Mrs S. Hurrell,
7 Weavers Drive, Glemsford, Suffolk, CO10 7SL.

Literature and collections

Both Standard and Triumph are thankfully well catered for when it comes to preserving their history. Documentation is maintained by the many clubs listed here, but there are a number of organisations and museums that have a strong collection of related material, including restored examples of the breeds.

The British Motor Industry Heritage Trust, which now has a permanent purpose-built museum in Gaydon, have build records for the later cars as well as a number of complete vehicles which will be displayed in due course.

The Museum of British Road Transport based in Coventry has a fine collection of Standard and Triumph machines, covering, in both cases, the complete history of the company. The earliest surviving Standard, registered SMC 1, is on display at Coventry, and in all, around twenty Standard and Triumph cars can be seen at any one time. There is also a collection of Triumph cycles and the legendary Triumph motorcycles housed there.

The National Motor Museum at Beaulieu has a number of important machines, and like Coventry Museum and the Warwick University, a superb collection of historical photographs and documents, etc.

As far as books are concerned, a collection of articles and brochures; one covering pre-war Standard Cars, the other covering the postwar models, are available from the Standard Motor Club, and there are literally dozens of excellent Triumph books for the more dedicated enthusiast.

INDEX

Dear Reader,
We hope you enjoyed this Veloce
Publishing production.
If you have ideas for other books on
Standard/Standard-Triumph, or any
other marque, please write and tell
us.
Meantime, Happy Motoring!

THE END